access to religion and philosophy

a
t
r
p

Religion and Science SECOND EDITION

Mel Thompson

WITHDRAWN

D0314530

11. 2008

HODDER
EDUCATION
PART OF HACHETTE LIVRE UK

UNIVERSITY OF CHICHESTER

The Publishers would like to thank the following for permission to reproduce copyright material:

Photo credits

Cover © STScl/NASA/Corbis; all other images © Mel Thompson

Acknowledgements

p130 SCM Press for the quote from *Taking Leave of God* by Don Cupitt (SCM Press, 1980)

Every effort has been made to trace all copyright holders, but if any have been inadvertently overlooked the Publishers will be pleased to make the necessary arrangements at the first opportunity.

Although every effort has been made to ensure that website addresses are correct at time of going to press, Hodder Education cannot be held responsible for the content of any website mentioned in this book. It is sometimes possible to find a relocated web page by typing in the address of the home page for a website in the URL window of your browser.

Hachette's policy is to use papers that are natural, renewable and recyclable products and made from wood grown in sustainable forests. The logging and manufacturing processes are expected to conform to the environmental regulations of the country of origin.

Orders: please contact Bookpoint Ltd, 130 Milton Park, Abingdon, Oxon OX14 4SB. Telephone: +44 (0)1235 827720. Fax: +44 (0)1235 400454. Lines are open 9.00a.m.–5.00p.m., Monday to Saturday, with a 24-hour message answering service. Visit our website at www.hoddereducation.co.uk

© Mel Thompson 2000, 2008

First edition published 2000

This second edition first published in 2008
by Hodder Education,
part of Hachette Livre UK
338 Euston Road
London NW1 3BH

Impression number   5 4 3 2 1

Year   2012 2011 2010 2009 2008

All rights reserved. Apart from any use permitted under UK copyright law, no part of this publication may be reproduced or transmitted in any form or by any means, electronic or mechanical, including photocopying and recording, or held within any information storage and retrieval system, without permission in writing from the publisher or under licence from the Copyright Licensing Agency Limited. Further details of such licences (for reprographic reproduction) may be obtained from the Copyright Licensing Agency Limited, Saffron House, 6–10 Kirby Street, London EC1N 8TS.

Illustrations by GreenGate Publishing Services
Typeset in Bembo by GreenGate Publishing Services, Tonbridge, Kent
Printed in Great Britain by Martins the Printers, Berwick-upon-Tweed

A catalogue record for this title is available from the British Library

ISBN: 978 0340 95776 9

CR
215
THO

CONTENTS

PREFACE

To the student

Access books are written mainly for students studying for examinations at higher level, particularly GCE Advanced Subsidiary (AS) level and Advanced (A) level. A number of features have been included to assist students, such as the study guides at the end of chapters.

To use these books most effectively, you should be aware of the following features:

- At the beginning of each chapter there is a checklist, which is a brief introduction about the key elements that the chapter covers.
- Key questions, words, people, thoughts and quotes in the margin highlight specific points from the main text.
- Profiles of key individuals give information on a philosopher's background and work.
- There are summary diagrams throughout the chapters to aid revision.
- The revision checklist at the end of each chapter summarises the main points.

General advice on answering essay questions

Structured questions will tell you what to include. The following advice is for those questions which leave it to you to work out:

- The most important thing is to read the question carefully and work out what it really means. Make sure you understand all the words in the question (you may need to check some of them in the dictionary or look up technical terms in the glossary at the back of this book).
- Gather the relevant information for answering the question. You will probably not need everything you know on the topic. Keep to what the question is asking.
- Organise your material by drawing up a plan of paragraphs. Make sure that each paragraph is relevant to the question. Include different views within your answer (most questions require arguments for and against).
- Start with an introduction that explains in your own words what the question is asking and defines any technical words. Work through your answer in carefully planned paragraphs. Write a brief conclusion in which you sum up your answer to the question (without repeating everything in the essay).

INTRODUCTION

The view of the world offered by science is awe inspiring, and the sheer dimensions of the universe, revealed by astronomy, stretch our imagination. At one extreme, particle physics explores forces within the atom; at the other, telescopes looking deep into space provide evidence of events that took place so long ago that the light from them started its journey towards us even before our planet was formed. The complexity of things we take for granted, like the amount of genetic information needed to construct a human body, is quite astounding. So when it comes to developing a sense of wonder and the challenge to understand who we are within this universe, science provides a good starting point.

Science also challenges our assumptions. It is a discipline that deliberately examines and questions evidence. What may seem obvious to one generation is questioned by the next. And, by doing so, science works its way towards a total understanding of the world – an ultimate goal that (in practical terms) it will probably never be able to fulfil, but which remains the spur for ever more questioning and exploration.

Life without science and technology would be unthinkable for most people in the developed world. Deprived of modern medicine, transport or communications, our lifestyle would be severely impaired. Nobody seriously doubts the value of what science contributes, but that does not mean that science meets every human need; the arts, personal relationships, emotional fulfilment, a sense of purpose: these are equally important for human happiness, but they are not directly addressed by scientific theory, nor do they depend on technology.

There is also much represented by the term 'religion' that science does not address: intuitions about the meaning and purpose of life, a sense of being 'at home' in the universe, and convictions about what is morally right.

Clearly, science has not replaced religion. A majority of people still claim to belong, at least nominally, to one of the major world religions, and even where interest in organised religion is in decline, the intuitions about life and its meaning, the sense of wonder and of celebration, which in previous generations would have been expressed largely through the medium of religion, are still very much in evidence.

Key quote

The eventual goal of science is to provide a single theory that describes the whole universe.
STEPHEN HAWKING, *A BRIEF HISTORY OF TIME*, 1988

Key question

Do religion and science offer complementary views, or does the scientific world view automatically exclude religious belief?

Sadly, however, much of the debate between science and religion in recent years has been between those who hold extreme positions. On the one hand there are religious fundamentalists, who take it as an article of faith that every word of the Bible should be taken out of its original context and understood as literal or scientific truth. On the other, there are some scientists who appear blind to the significance of anything that cannot be quantified and expressed in scientific terms, and who delight in caricaturing and dismissing religious belief. But – as we shall see later – it is fundamentally wrong to treat religious beliefs as though they were bad science (although some religious fundamentalists, just like their scientific critics, try to do just that); and it is equally wrong to treat science as though it were a religion, answering all human problems and needs.

But there is another aspect to the dialogue between religion and science, for religion is a phenomenon like any other, and as such it may be examined and explained. Religion is not limited to a set of propositions – the beliefs that religious people hold to be true – but is a way of life, sustained for many reasons, not least the sense of shared purpose or social solidarity that it can offer. So part of what science can do is to examine the phenomenon of religion, why it exists at all and what part it plays in human life.

Our task in this book is to look at these two very important aspects of human life and see how they are related to one another. But those who expect a book to conclude either that science has made all forms of religion redundant, or that religion can somehow prove science wrong, are likely to be disappointed. The matter is not that simple.

1 The interface of religion and science

It is possible to define the areas of interest of religion and science in such a way that they do not conflict with one another. In 1925, A. N. Whitehead suggested:

Key thought

Stephen Jay Gould (1941–2002) argued for a 'non-overlapping magisteria' between science and religion. In other words, science and religion each possess the appropriate tools for dealing with their particular aspects of life: science deals with the physical world; religion deals with issues of meaning, value and morality. Problems occur when they step outside their appropriate realm and try to comment on each other.

Science is concerned with the general conditions which are observed to regulate physical phenomena; whereas religion is wholly wrapped up in the contemplation of moral and aesthetic values. On the one side there is the law of gravitation, and on the other the contemplation of the beauty of holiness. What one side sees, the other misses; and vice versa.
(*Science and the Modern World*)

But this view (which has a long history) does not do justice to the fact that both religion and science offer an overall way of understanding the world. Science, in setting out the general conditions of physical phenomena, thereby makes claims about the

Key word

Normative: one way of describing the relationship between science and religion is to say that science is *descriptive* while religion is *normative*. Normative issues concern the 'norms' or values by which things may be judged. Ethics is normative when it argues that particular things are right or wrong. Politics is normative when it claims to show the best way of running a nation. Religion is normative when it speaks of the value of the world and of things within it, rather than simply describing what exists.

Key quote

Religion is concerned with man's attitude toward nature at large, with the establishing of ideals for the individual and communal life, and with mutual human relationships.
ALBERT EINSTEIN, 1948, IN *IDEAS AND OPINIONS*, 1954

Key thought

We need to distinguish between the propositions that some religious people hold to be true (e.g. that God exists; that miracles can violate laws of nature; that people can survive death) and the phenomena of religion (e.g. the fact that people gather together and take part in religious rituals, prayer, celebration and so on). Most of the conflicts between science and religion have come about because religious beliefs, often taken out of context, appear to contradict scientific views of the nature of the world.

Cross-reference

For an approach to this problem within the philosophy of religion, see 'The parable of the gardener' in: *Philosophy and Ethics*, page 92; *The Philosophy of Religion*, page 151.

nature of the world and of life that are relevant to human beings and their religious impulses. Equally, religion is seldom prepared to limit what it says to the areas of morality and aesthetics.

Religion is a very broad term; we need to be more specific. Some religions have no problem with science. Buddhism, for example, is based on the investigation of phenomena, and is not dogmatic. It has a view of the world that corresponds very closely to the modern scientific view, and where it appears to make claims that science might challenge, it offers them only as guidelines, not as dogmas to be accepted without question.

On the other hand, the Western theistic religions – Judaism, Christianity and Islam – are all dogmatic, in that they have doctrines to which believers are required to subscribe. A person cannot, for example, be regarded as a Christian without beliefs (whether expressed conservatively or radically) in the existence of God, the divinity and resurrection of Christ, and the hope of eternal life or personal resurrection. Equally, it would be difficult to be Christian and not accept the idea of miracles or the effectiveness of prayer. Radical theologians may try to re-interpret doctrines to make them compatible with modern world views, but such interpretations are by no means universally accepted. To be a believer requires a commitment to accept certain things as true, and to see the world as created by God. A similar case could be made for both Judaism and Islam, for both are grounded in a belief in God which has enormous implications for understanding oneself and the world.

What is more, all the major religions speak of a fundamental reality, which they see as underlying everything we experience:

- *Torah* (Law) – in Judaism
- *Logos* (Word) – in Christianity
- *Shariah* (Law) – in Islam
- *Dharma* (Reality or Teaching) – in Hinduism
- *Shunyata* (Emptiness) – in Mahayana Buddhism.

In other words, they claim to be dealing with, and to be based on, something fundamental to the way the world is. This inevitably brings them, and their claims, into the scientific arena.

Things are detected in science by the difference that they make. The bending of light shows the presence of a strong gravitational field; the presence of disease is suggested by the failure of one or more of the body's organs to work normally. It is therefore reasonable for a scientist to examine whether 'God' makes any difference, as a way of deciding whether or not he exists.

Students of the philosophy of religion may recall the well-known story about two explorers who, coming across a clearing in the jungle with a mixture of flowers and weeds, debate whether or not it is tended by a gardener. Famously, it is argued that the hypothesis that there is a gardener 'dies the death of a thousand qualifications' as each test for his presence proves negative.

In his recent book *God: The Failed Hypothesis*, Victor Stenger takes just this approach, arguing that science is in a position to check the sort of evidence that would be expected to account for the existence of God. As the 'explorers story' illustrates, religious believers are seldom convinced by such an argument, for belief in God is not a simple question about the existence of a physical object. Believers would claim that God can be said to exist, even though they would admit that he does not have a physical body, and so cannot be tested for in the way that might be applied to other things.

So one of the tasks of 'religion and science' is to explore and *sensitise* each side of what can become a confrontational debate to the subtleties of scientific method on one side and the different forms of belief and religious intuition on the other. The failure of communication can otherwise lead to a rather sad pair of caricatures – with the nihilist, insensitive scientist on the one side, and a naïve believer who accepts a crudely conceived, quasi-physical deity on the other.

> **Key quote**
>
> *Science without religion is lame, religion without science is blind.*
> ALBERT EINSTEIN, *SCIENCE, RELIGION AND PHILOSOPHY: A SYMPOSIUM,* 1941

In fact, as Einstein and others have so eloquently shown, there are a richness and mystery in life that embrace both religion and science in a quest for knowledge and a sense of wonder.

2 Change and commitment

Nobody would dream of saying that science was threatened or destroyed by the new ideas put forward by Einstein or Darwin. Rather, these thinkers represent a step forward for science. Well established theories are tested out and modified, and eventually they may need to be scrapped and replaced: that is the way science makes progress. With religion, however, many beliefs are held for very deeply personal reasons, or because they express the identity of a particular group of people. Challenges to those beliefs are therefore often resisted.

The nature of commitment is also different. In religion, commitment is often made to a particular belief, or even more narrowly to a particular way of expressing a belief, a form of words or a creed. In science, the commitment is to the scientific quest itself, and to its established method of examining evidence, rather than to any one particular theory. Here again, we come up against a fundamental difference between religion and science.

> **Key thought**
>
> Of course, there are cases of scientists becoming committed to particular theories, but, in the long run, science is based on evidence, and a scientist who holds a view that goes against that evidence is likely to be challenged for acting in an 'unscientific' way.

But to appreciate this difference, it is important to examine the debates between religion and science in their historical context. Christianity originated at a time when people's view of the world was very different from that revealed by modern science. Ideas about God, the supernatural, miracles or demonic forces as the cause of illness, unremarkable 2000 years ago, may cause problems for people today.

Those who shaped the early doctrines of the Church were influenced by the best available philosophy of their day; Augustine of Hippo was deeply impressed by neo-Platonic thought and the thirteenth-century theologian Aquinas used the newly rediscovered ideas of Aristotle. Their ideas were therefore closely linked with the general views of their time.

The problem with this is that ideas and philosophies of a previous age become embedded in scriptures and creeds and arguments, and therefore *appear to be endorsed by religious authority.* Thus the new interpretations of the universe (e.g. from Galileo) appeared to conflict with the philosophical views of Aristotle. But those views had become so intertwined with Christian doctrine that an attack on Aristotle appeared to be an attack on religion itself.

With the Renaissance and Reformation, the authority of religious doctrines was challenged, enabling secular philosophy and science to emerge, although often through the work of those who would have described themselves as religious. By the eighteenth century, philosophers like Hume could question the evidence for miracles in a radical way. His arguments were not science, but they were made possible because of an environment in which it was natural to question such things.

Religion has responded in a number of ways to the challenge of science. Some Christians have argued that the Bible must be right and therefore science (if it disagrees) must be wrong. Hence there are those who try to show that the world was created as described in Genesis. Others have tried to reinterpret Christianity in ways that show its beliefs to be compatible with science.

Such reinterpretations are not new, nor are they necessarily disloyal to the Christian tradition. A first-century Christian would have struggled to understand the views of Aquinas (in the thirteenth century) and would have been totally incredulous when faced with the kind of mechanical world accepted by Christians in the eighteenth century as proof of God's creative design. *The outrageous heresy of one generation may well become the accepted belief for the next.*

Key thought

Few Christians today would want to argue that the Sun revolves around the Earth, or that, by divine influence, blood seeps from one side of the heart to the other, but at one time they might have felt obliged to do so!

3 Relevance

Science has not always adequately explained or explored its relevance. Professor Erwin Schrödinger (most widely known for his illustration of one of the dilemmas of quantum theory in a puzzle known as 'Schrödinger's cat'; see page 56) offered a sound piece of advice to scientists in a lecture given in 1950:

> *Never lose sight of the role your particular subject has within the great performance of the tragi-comedy of human life; keep in touch with life – not so much with practical life as with the ideal background of life, which is ever so much more important; and,* keep life in touch with you. *If you cannot – in the long run – tell everyone what you have been doing, your doing has been worthless.*
>
> (E. Schrödinger, *Science and Humanism*, 1950)

But equally, religion has sometimes focused too narrowly on doctrinal formulae, and set aside the breadth of its spiritual quest. A. N. Whitehead put it thus:

> *Religion is the vision of something which stands beyond, behind, and within, the passing flux of immediate things; something which is real, and yet waiting to be realised; something which is a remote possibility, and yet the greatest of present facts; something that gives meaning to all that passes, and yet eludes apprehension; something whose possession is the final goal, and yet is beyond all reach; something which is the ultimate ideal, and the hopeless quest.*
>
> (*Science and the Modern World*, 1925)

Whitehead thus saw religion as an overall, integrating, personal view of life, giving meaning and purpose to the ever-changing multiplicity of things.

Those engaged in science may benefit from exploring the general questions about meaning and purpose that are raised by religion. This is particularly true in terms of the ethical and environmental consequences of scientific advances, for example. Without some sense of direction or purpose, science loses its impetus. It has been argued that one should seek knowledge for knowledge's sake. In practice this has almost never been the case for very long. Knowledge has quickly been utilised for other purposes, whether for weapons of war, or new medical techniques.

But equally, it would be most unwise for religious believers to try to keep their beliefs separated off from the general understanding of the world that informs everyday life. For its own health, it needs to be informed by, and even challenged by, science.

Key thought

The approach to philosophy known as 'pragmatism' judges ideas by the relevance and value they have for us. Their function is to help us solve problems. We may not know whether they are true in an absolute sense, but we can say whether or not they work for us. This applies to scientific theories (where a theory is judged by the useful predictions it makes) but it can equally be applied to religious beliefs. We should ask not just 'What does it *say*?' but also 'What does it *do*?', 'What *difference* does this idea or belief make?' Things that make no difference are irrelevant, even if they are true.

The objects of religious belief (e.g. God) are regarded by religious people as relevant; if they were not, there would be no point in religion. But how can that relevance be tested out? A scientific approach to this would involve devising various hypotheses in the form of 'If God exists, then X', where 'X' is something that can be observed or experienced and measured. If God's existence leaves no discernible trace, then it will be regarded as unlikely. A God who makes no difference is a God that cannot be detected, and hence a God who appears both improbable and irrelevant.

Hence it is important for both science and religion to specify carefully what they are doing and what they are claiming.

But we need to keep in mind the sense of wonder that science can encourage. At the end of *The Origin of Species*, Darwin spoke of the 'grandeur' of the view of life that he had outlined (see page 85). Almost 140 years later, a modern exponent of Darwin, having noted how lucky we all are to be alive (given the much larger possibility that we would never have been born), put it thus:

> *It is no accident that our kind of life finds itself on a planet whose temperature, rainfall and everything else are exactly right. If the planet were suitable for another kind of life, it is that other kind of life that would have evolved here. But we as individuals are still hugely blessed. Privileged, and not just privileged to enjoy our planet. More, we are granted the opportunity to understand why our eyes are open, and why they see what they do, in the short time before they close forever …*
>
> *After sleeping through a hundred million centuries we have finally opened our eyes on a sumptuous planet, sparkling with colour, bountiful with life. Within decades we must close our eyes again. Isn't it a noble, an enlightened way of spending our brief time in the sun, to work at understanding the universe and how we have come to wake up in it?*
>
> (Richard Dawkins, *Unweaving the Rainbow*, 1998)

That seems to me to be one of the clearest expressions of the deeply spiritual or religious impulse behind the best of science. Science is not just about solving problems, it is also a deep quest for understanding the nature of reality and our place within it.

FROM THE GREEKS TO THE MEDIEVAL WORLD

Chapter checklist

As background to the issues of science and religion, we look at the earliest scientific explorations of the Greeks, at Plato and Aristotle, and finally at the medieval world view which dominated Western religious thinking prior to the rise of modern science.

For 1500 years, the Christian view of the world had been so influenced by the Greek philosophers Plato and Aristotle that their ideas and those of Christianity had seemed inseparable. Their thought provided an intellectual structure within which Christian doctrines were expressed and through which they were defended.

1 Pre-Socratic theories

The earliest Greek philosophers (generally known as the 'pre-Socratics' since they taught before the very influential period of Socrates, Plato and Aristotle) were concerned to develop general theories to explain the nature of things.

The earliest of these, Thales (sixth century BCE), came to the remarkable view that all matter (substances of very different sorts, solid or liquid) was ultimately reducible to a single element, and mistakenly (although understandably, considering how widespread it is) thought this element was water. What was remarkable was not his conclusion but his quest – the idea that everything can be analysed to find a common element.

Equally astounding was the insight of Heraclitus (also sixth century BCE) that everything is in a state of flux: things may appear to be permanent, but in fact everything is subject to change.

Leucippus and Democritus (fifth century BCE) developed a theory known as **atomism**, which suggested that all matter was comprised of very small particles separated by empty space. This,

Key quote

You cannot step into the same river twice.

HERACLITUS

Key word

Atomism: the theory that all matter is composed of atoms separated by empty space.

remarkable in its anticipation of modern science, implied that individual things, and the materials of which they were made, took on their character by the form or organisation of the atoms of which they were comprised. In other words, here was a theory of matter that saw different sorts of substance as representing various combinations of a single basic feature, the atom.

They saw that substances can change – water becoming ice or steam – and recognised this as evidence for a common atomic basis for all three. It is difficult to overemphasise what a remarkable achievement this was. Moving from observation to the formulation of an underlying theory, *these pre-Socratic philosophers were doing what we would clearly recognise as science* – they were asking fundamental questions, examining evidence and seeking a rational explanation.

2 Plato

Key people

Plato (c.428–347BCE)
Plato was born into a noble family in Athens and was profoundly influenced by the philosopher Socrates. When Socrates was condemned to death in 399BCE, Plato left Athens for twelve years, returning to found the Academy, where he received students at his home. His philosophy makes a radical distinction between those things that are experienced through the senses and the eternal realities known through reason.

Key word

Form: Plato's term for a universal, of which particulars are merely copies.

Key thoughts

Plato's idea of the 'forms' suggests that eternal universals are more real than the concrete particulars that exhibit them.

At heart, many disagreements between science and religion go back to the adoption by religious believers of this Platonic assumption that the 'real' is beyond the realm of the senses, and hence beyond what science can show.

Plato argued that the things we see and experience around us are only copies of unseen eternal realities. Thus the tree that I see in front of me is a particular example of an ideal, perfect tree. I know it to be a tree because I have an intuition of that ideal tree – indeed, it is the eternal and ideal tree that leads us to the notion 'tree' in the first place. Therefore, in order to understand the world, a person has to look *beyond* the particular and examine the most general and universal.

In his famous analogy of the cave, most people do not see things as they really are, but merely a set of fleeting images, shadows cast on a wall as objects are passed in front of a fire. The philosopher sees beyond the fire, through the mouth of the cave, to the light of the sun. Reality is understood only by turning away from the wall and its shadows (the phenomena we experience) and make a difficult journey out of the cave and into the world of eternal and unchanging **forms**.

The key feature here is that there are two very different worlds, the world of the forms, ideal and perfect, and the imperfect, transient world of our everyday experience. The religious person, like the philosopher, is encouraged to turn away from the latter in order to appreciate the former.

Notice what far-reaching implications this has for religion and science. For Plato, the concept or idea is more real than the particular things experienced. As Christianity became influenced by Platonic thought, it therefore claimed that its doctrines represented a reality, compared with which knowledge of this world was but a pale shadow. This is the very opposite of the scientific approach, which is empirical – i.e. it is based on experience.

3 Aristotle

Key people

Aristotle (384–322BCE)
Hugely influential Greek thinker. He considered everything to have an essence, which was shown by a rational interpretation of its purpose or end. He criticised Plato's idea of the forms, and placed evidence and reason at the heart of his theory of knowledge, and was concerned to study and classify natural things, thus paving the way for science.

Key words

Efficient cause: that which is the agent of change.
Final cause: the purpose, or product, of a process of change.

Key thought

If someone has fallen seriously ill, a person who believes in God may ask 'Why has this happened?' Clearly, he or she is not expecting an answer in terms of *efficient causality* (in other words, about virus infection or other medical conditions), but *final causality*: not what conditions have brought about the illness, but what its purpose is. In other words, the person is expecting that the illness will have some final cause, perhaps in order to teach someone something, or to give them an opportunity to display certain qualities. The more tragic and pointless the suffering, the more difficult it becomes to see that it has a 'final cause'. This is the basis of the religious 'problem of evil'.

Aristotle took a very different approach from that of Plato. He argued that our knowledge of the world comes through experience interpreted by reason. In other words, you need to examine phenomena, not turn away from them.

In line with this view, it was Aristotle who classified the different sciences. He also introduced the term 'metaphysics' for those sections in his work that came after those on physics – and these were the ones that dealt with the more general issues of the structure of thought, as opposed to the examination of experience.

The process of scientific thinking therefore owes more to Aristotle than to Plato, although, as we shall see later, the authority given to Aristotle's ideas was a hindrance to the development of science. The basic assumption about how knowledge is gained, and the relationship between things perceived and the more general ideas to which they give rise (i.e. the distinction between science and metaphysics), stem from Aristotle.

a) The four causes

Aristotle considered that things had four different types of causes. These are best appreciated by considering the example of someone chipping away at a block of stone in order to produce a sculpture:

1. The stone itself is the *material cause* of the sculpture.
2. The emerging shape of the chipped stone is the *formal cause* of the sculpture.
3. The person chipping away is the **efficient cause** of the sculpture.
4. The sculpture itself is the **final cause** of what is taking place. It represents the purpose and intention behind the activity of the sculptor in doing the work.

Of these, the *efficient cause* is the one most often considered; indeed, in ordinary language, to cause something is to be the agent of bringing it about.

For Christian ideas about God, however, the idea of a *final cause* became important, for it suggested that everything had its place and purpose in God's final plan.

It is important to recognise that, for Aristotle, *all four* causes were included in the description of an object. When we come to look at the rise of modern science in the seventeenth century we shall see that the universe was thought of as a huge, impersonal mechanism, operating according to fixed laws. These laws considered material objects, their relations to one another and the forces operating upon them. It tended to overlook the idea of purpose in its analysis, relegating it to a more general idea of the purpose given by an external creator God.

Hence, it was the exclusion of Aristotle's 'final causes' from its analysis that led science to relegate questions of meaning and purpose to the realm of religion.

b) Unmoved movers

Aristotle argued that everything was caused by something else, which in turn was caused by yet something else again. But can you have an infinite sequence of causes? In theory it is possible, but in practice you can never know that a sequence is infinite: the most you can say is that it *appears* to have no end. Thus there are no actual infinities, only theoretical ones.

Therefore Aristotle's philosophy leaves open the possibility of an unmoved mover (or uncaused cause), responsible for all movement in the universe, and the cause of all that exists. However, it would be equally possible for the world to be infinite and eternal – needing no uncaused cause, because it would have no starting point and no boundary.

The thirteenth-century philosopher and theologian, Thomas Aquinas, was to use Aristotle's argument about the possibility of an unmoved mover to present his cosmological argument for the existence of God. But whereas Aristotle could conceive of an infinite world, Aquinas could not. For his view was that, if the world were infinite and eternal, there would be no need to posit a creator – indeed the idea of creation makes no sense if the world is eternal. Aquinas could not accept that possibility, and therefore opted for the idea of the uncaused cause.

> **Key thought**
>
> For Aristotle and the other philosophers of this period, there was no distinction between philosophy and science. Reason applied to experience was both science and philosophy. Indeed, it was only with its increasing specialisation that science became separated from philosophy. Until the nineteenth century, physics was generally called 'natural philosophy', a term still found today in some traditional university departments.

4 Shaping the medieval world view

> **Key thought**
>
> It was the combination of Greek thought, Ptolemaic cosmology and Christian doctrine that provided the view of the world that was endorsed by religious authority, but was challenged by the rise of science.

a) Ptolemy of Alexandria (second century CE)

Medieval Christian culture had a view of the world that was based partly on biblical imagery and partly on a mixture of the views of Plato, Aristotle and the cosmology of Ptolemy of Alexandria.

In that cosmology, Earth was at the centre of the universe, surrounded by glassy spheres on which were located the moving planets and the fixed stars. There were ten spheres in all, seven for the known heavenly bodies, an eighth for the stars, an invisible ninth which moved the others, and a tenth which was the abode of God.

All movement was controlled by spiritual forces, and this led to an interest in astrology, since each sphere was thought to influence events on the Earth. Everything in the spheres above the Moon was perfect and unchanging. God's power was believed to filter down to Earth through the influence of these heavenly bodies.

Key people

Ptolemy of Alexandria (c.100–170)
A major scientist and philosopher of his time, Ptolemy was particularly influenced by Aristotle, and clarified the process by which basic observations lead to scientific theories. His cosmology reflected earlier views about the nature of perfection.

Key words

Deduction: the process of applying logic in order to establish conclusions from general principles.
Induction: the process of gathering data from observation and experiment in order to establish a general theory or principle.

Key people

St Augustine of Hippo (354–430)
Born in North Africa to a Christian mother and pagan father, Augustine was a philosopher, rising to become a teacher of rhetoric in the imperial court in Milan, Italy. There he converted to Christianity and returned to Africa where he was ordained and became a bishop. His thinking reflects a blending of philosophy, biblical studies and Christian doctrine.

Key quote

Let no one think that, because the Psalmist says, He established the earth above the water, *we must use this testimony of Holy Scripture against these people who engage in learned discussions about the weight of the elements. They are not bound by the authority of our Bible; and, ignorant of the sense of these words, they will more readily scorn our sacred books than disavow the knowledge they have acquired by unassailable arguments or proved by the evidence of experience.*
ST AUGUSTINE, *THE LITERAL MEANING OF GENESIS*, VOLUME 1

The Earth itself was thought to be made up of four elements – earth, water, air and fire – each of which had a natural level, with earth sinking down and fire rising up. So motion was explained in terms of the natural tendency of the elements.

There was also a distinction between motion on Earth and that in the heavens. The heavens were perfect, and motion therefore had to follow a perfect form – namely, it had to be circular. This belief was later to prove an obstacle to scientists, not merely in the view that planetary motion had to be circular, but also by opposing the idea put forward by Harvey that blood was pumped around the body by the heart. Such circular movement of blood could not be accepted as true, for circular motion was only appropriate in the heavenly realms, not on Earth!

Notice that such arguments were the product of **deduction**. In other words, they started with a theory and then examined what facts ought to follow from it. Contrast this with an argument produced by **induction**, as used by science, where evidence is gathered and a theory framed in order to explain it.

b) St Augustine (354–430)

St Augustine was a hugely influential Christian writer, but for our purposes we need to notice just two things that particularly influence later issues in religion and science:

- He was convinced that, since God was the creator, something of his nature should be seen within his creation – even though that creation was 'fallen'. In particular he saw God reflected in what he considered to be the highest feature of the created order: human reason.
- The second, which was taken up by Aquinas and others, was that the wonder people feel in examining the natural world should lead on naturally to a worship of God, its creator.

These, as we shall see, are basic to what is known as the 'argument from design'. Taken together they imply a view of the world as rational and purposeful, and which moves from rationality, beauty and purpose to an acknowledgement of the existence and creativity of God. But the divine order is quite separate from the ever-changing material realm. Like Plato, he makes a clear distinction between the eternal and the temporal.

But St Augustine's writings are relevant to the religion and science debate for quite another reason. He was concerned that an interpretation of scripture should not be presented in a way that ran counter to reason and evidence. He was afraid that such interpretations might result in the scriptures being scorned. This is most instructive, since it comes from a period before the rise of science as we know it today, but shows that the issue of taking a

Key thought

In 529CE, the Emperor Justinian outlawed the teaching of philosophy, in the interests of an empire unified by Christianity. Hence the works of Aristotle were largely unknown in the West, until (via translations from the Arabic into Latin) they were studied once more in universities in Europe in the thirteenth century. An interesting example of the restriction placed on science – or natural philosophy – in the interests of religion and politics.

literalist view of the scriptural texts could be an embarrassment in terms of explaining the significance of Christianity to those outside the faith. The terms used may have changed since his day, but the folly of interpreting the scriptures as though they presented literal, scientific facts, counter to those established by the scientific method, remains the same.

c) The Kalam argument

Until the thirteenth century, the works of Aristotle were not widely known in the Christian West. His re-introduction into mainstream Christian thinking took place only with the work of Aquinas (see below). But before that time, an argument for the existence of God was developed by the Muslim philosophers al-Kindi (ninth century) and al-Ghazali (eleventh century), which reflects the philosophy of Aristotle, which had been preserved in Arabic translation.

The argument may be set out as follows:

- Everything that begins to exist must have a cause for its existence.
- The universe began to exist.
- Therefore the universe must have had a cause.

This argument is based on the idea that, although you can have a theoretical infinite, you cannot have an actual infinite. It is impossible to show an infinite succession of causes, stretching back into the past. At some point, it was argued, there must have been a situation where the universe either could have or could not have come into existence. But al-Ghazali argued that in situations where one of two things can happen, neither being absolutely determined, what actually happens will depend upon the will and choice of a personal agent. This agent must be God.

The Kalam approach is interesting from the perspective of the philosophy of religion, but it also has implications for a consideration of the relationship between religion and science. For Islam, Allah is the supreme creative source of everything, omnipotent and omnipresent. What the Kalam argument says is that we cannot continue a series of causal explanations for ever. Therefore, although individual things within the universe can be explained in terms of causes that precede them, the universe itself cannot be so explained, but must come through the personal choice of God.

Not everyone would agree. One might argue that, where two possibilities are equally likely, things happen at random, without any personal choice, or that an actual infinity is possible, although we can never prove it. Or one might argue that causality is circular (perpetual motion), with the universe like the inner surface of a sphere, so that you can travel for ever, crossing and re-crossing your tracks, but never come to an end.

Key thought

Once you accept that God can be part of an explanation of the nature of the universe, then belief in him will predispose you to accept only those scientific explanations that back up such belief. That's not good science, but it does God no favours either, because if he's used in the wrong explanation, he'll be dismissed along with it.

Key people

Thomas Aquinas (1224/5–74)
Aquinas was born in Roccasecca, near Naples, was sent to be educated at the Abbey of Monte Cassino at the age of 5, and later studied at the universities of Naples, Cologne and Paris. He belonged to the Dominican order and was therefore committed to a life of study and preaching. His most important works are *Summa Theologiae* and *Summa contra Gentiles*.

Key thought

Aquinas used the analogy of an arrow speeding to its target. The arrow, being inanimate, cannot have intelligence or purpose. Therefore the purposive nature of its flight indicates the action of an intelligent archer.

But notice that what you have here is the insertion of a religious concept (God) into a logical argument about the structure of the universe. In other words, *God is used to explain the universe's structure*, and – once this is done – there is the danger that, for a person who wishes to continue to believe in God, there will be a temptation to accept only those explanations of the universe that give scope for God to have such a place.

d) Thomas Aquinas

The influence of Aquinas on subsequent Christian teaching, especially within the Roman Catholic Church, has been immense. He is best known for his 'five ways', put forward as arguments for the existence of God. In these he attempted to use concepts developed by Aristotle, especially his idea of final causes and of the uncaused cause, to show that a logical examination of agreed facts about the world led to the conclusion that God existed as an unmoved mover, uncaused cause.

Aquinas was fortunate in arriving at university at exactly the time when Aristotle's works were starting to be rediscovered again in the West, mostly translated from Arabic. Aquinas was therefore able to use what was considered to be the best natural philosophy of his day as a way of justifying and explaining his Christian beliefs.

In terms of this medieval synthesis of natural philosophy and Christian doctrine, it is probably the equivalent of a theologian today taking arguments about what happened at the 'Big Bang' to explain God in terms of the developing structure of the universe. Whatever is meant by 'God', in Aquinas' terms, is integral to his whole understanding of the structure of reality. In his thought there is no sudden move from natural philosophy to religion – the one leads on into the other.

Thus, for Aquinas, the exploration of the final cause of something – the natural purpose and function it has within the whole scheme of things – only serves to confirm his view of divine providence. If inanimate things were seen to work together for some purpose, that suggested that there must be a creator and designer to have organised that: God. Value and purpose – established through the use of the Aristotelian idea of things having a 'final cause' – are now given religious authority.

When the medieval person looked up to the stars, set in fixed crystalline spheres, he or she saw meaning and significance because the Earth was at the centre of the universe, and the life of mankind was the special object of God's concern.

Since Aristotle's 'unmoved mover', there has been the assumption that the universe has a cause and an explanation beyond itself. It lies behind the cosmological arguments of Aquinas, the eighteenth-century arguments about design, and the desire of

Key question

As we encounter the newly emerging sciences one question becomes central. Does this medieval world view square with the facts delivered by evidence and reason?

some religious thinkers to find a direction and rational purpose to evolutionary change.

A rational universe, established by an 'unmoved mover', protects the human mind against the despair and nihilism of a world where everything is a product of chance. It offers a sense of ultimate meaning and purpose to human life.

5 Religion and the rise of science

Key thoughts

The Christian religion provided a view of the natural order that encouraged the rise of science, but an authoritative attitude that hindered it.

These astronomers were struggling against a background of religious authority which gave Greek notions of perfection priority over observations and experimental evidence. In other words, the earlier medieval system of thought was 'deductive' – it deduced what should happen from its ideas, in contrast to the later 'inductive' method of getting to a theory from observations.

The circle is a symbol of perfection and eternity. But does that imply that all perfect things should be circular?

For Plato, the unseen 'forms' were more real than the individual things that could be known through the senses. This way of thinking (backed by religion) led to the idea that reason and the concepts of perfection could determine what existed, and that any observations which appeared to contradict this must automatically be wrong.

As we shall see in the next chapter, astronomy gives examples of this. Copernicus and later Galileo presented a view of the universe in which the Earth revolved around the Sun, rather than vice versa. Their view was opposed by those whose idea of the universe came from Ptolemy and in which the Earth was surrounded by glassy spheres – perfect shapes, conveying the Sun, Moon and planets in perfect circular motion. Their work was challenged (and Galileo condemned) not because their observations were found to be at fault, but because they had trusted their observations, rather than deciding beforehand what should be the case. When Kepler concluded that the orbit of Mars was elliptical rather than circular, his view was controversial because all heavenly motion was thought to be perfect, and therefore had to be circular – reflecting the perfect shape.

There were however exceptions to the tendency of thinkers in the medieval period to accept the logic of perfection and final causes. Among these was Roger Bacon, who based his work on observation, and criticised the tendency to accept authority or custom as a sole reason to believe something to be true, a view that caused great controversy in his day.

There are features of the medieval world view that are important for understanding the rise of science and its relationship to religion. The Christian religion, as expressed in the medieval synthesis, promoted the views that:

- The world is created good and is therefore worth examining. (In other words, it was not a totally other-worldly religion, despising the physical.)
- God had made the world in a rational and ordered way, and thus it is capable of being understood correctly by human reason.

Key people

Roger Bacon (1220–92)
Equally at home in the worlds of
science and religion, Bacon – a
Franciscan friar – was an empiricist
(in other words, he based
knowledge on experience) and set
out the basics of scientific method
and the evaluation of evidence. He
was also imaginative in the
application of science and his
work on optics led to the
invention of spectacles.

Key thought

Fire had an innate tendency to rise
up and water to flow down; acorns
found their final purpose in the oak
tree into which they might grow.
This was a philosophy that fitted
well with religion, since purpose
and essence were central to both.

This is the potential of the acorn. You
cannot fully understand the significance of
an acorn without being aware of what it can
become. So from Aristotle through the
whole medieval period, the question was not
just 'What is it?' but 'What is it *for*?'

- Nature should not be worshipped in itself. It is not holy and untouchable. Therefore it may be examined and, if necessary, changed.
- Humankind had been given the right to 'subdue the earth' in the book of Genesis, and this would justify the development of technologies for human advancement.

When we come to look at some of the figures prominent in the rise of science, we will find that many of them are religious. Indeed, when the Royal Society was formed, seventy per cent of its members were Puritans, for whom religion was of supreme importance. For them, Christian teachings provided impetus for and justification of their scientific work.

One important thing to notice, however, was that Christian theology in the medieval period had become wedded to the philosophy of Aristotle. In other words, those who were to defend Christian teaching against the rise of new science were actually defending an old natural philosophy against a new one, for an attack on Aristotle appeared to imply an attack on Christian teaching itself.

Notice also that medieval thought, following the rediscovery of the works of Aristotle (whose philosophy was taught in universities throughout Europe from about 1250), was based on looking at *essences* and *potentials*. You asked what the essence of something was, and you then asked about its final purpose, how it could make its potential into something actual. The world was not (as in later centuries) seen as a collection of matter pushed and pulled by various forces, but as a collection of things created with a particular essence and seeking their final purpose and fulfilment.

Although it is tempting to contrast the medieval world with that of the rise of science in the seventeenth and eighteenth centuries, it would be a mistake to underestimate the way in which medieval thinkers and institutions made later science possible. The thirteenth century in particular saw a great flowering of philosophy and science, and the establishment of universities throughout Europe, with 'natural philosophy' taught within their faculties of arts, was an important preparation for later developments in both philosophy and science.

Summary diagram

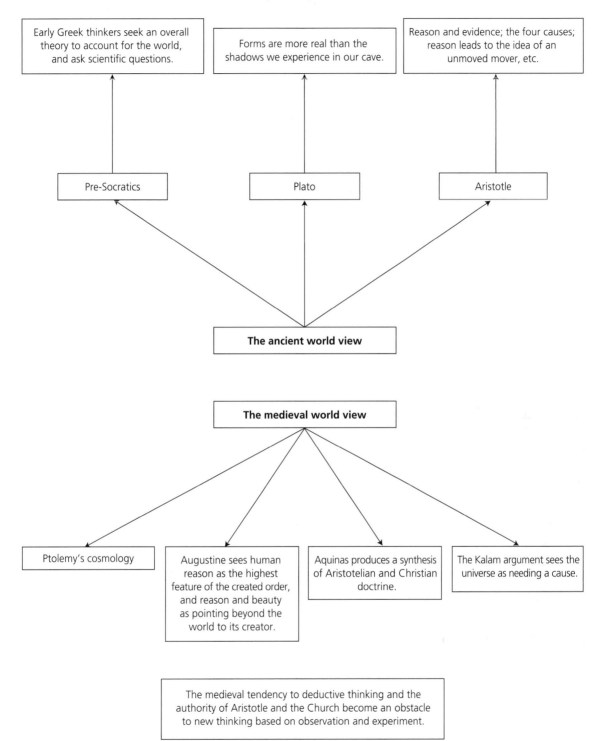

Early Greek thinkers seek an overall theory to account for the world, and ask scientific questions.

Forms are more real than the shadows we experience in our cave.

Reason and evidence; the four causes; reason leads to the idea of an unmoved mover, etc.

Pre-Socratics

Plato

Aristotle

The ancient world view

The medieval world view

Ptolemy's cosmology

Augustine sees human reason as the highest feature of the created order, and reason and beauty as pointing beyond the world to its creator.

Aquinas produces a synthesis of Aristotelian and Christian doctrine.

The Kalam argument sees the universe as needing a cause.

The medieval tendency to deductive thinking and the authority of Aristotle and the Church become an obstacle to new thinking based on observation and experiment.

Study guide

By the end of this chapter you should appreciate the mixture of Aristotle's philosophy, religious authority and a genuine attempt to argue for an overall meaning and purpose that constituted the medieval world view.

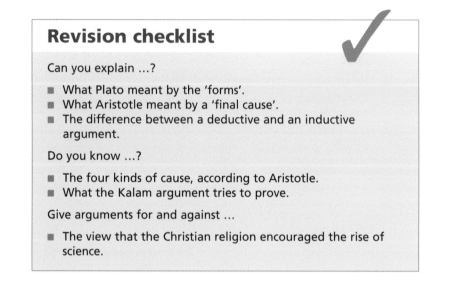

Revision checklist

Can you explain ...?

- What Plato meant by the 'forms'.
- What Aristotle meant by a 'final cause'.
- The difference between a deductive and an inductive argument.

Do you know ...?

- The four kinds of cause, according to Aristotle.
- What the Kalam argument tries to prove.

Give arguments for and against ...

- The view that the Christian religion encouraged the rise of science.

Examples of essay questions

A01

Select and demonstrate clearly relevant knowledge and understanding.

A02

Sustain a critical line of argument and justify a point of view.

1. Compare and contrast the philosophies of Plato and Aristotle in terms of their influence on the medieval world view and the religion of the period. Did they provide a help or a hindrance to the rise of science?

AO1 This requires a description of Plato's tendency to look for an ideal and universal, rather than at the objects of experience, contrasted with Aristotle's philosophy based on reason and evidence, but also his drive to understand 'final causes', and his influence on Aquinas.

AO2 This requires a balance between seeing how this philosophy enabled science to ask the right questions, and understanding the problem of authority, and therefore the resistance to new evidence or reasoning.

2. Does the medieval world view require the existence of God in order to make sense?

AO1 The key facts here concern Aristotle's and Aquinas' views of the uncaused cause, etc., which were taken to explain how the universe came into being and is sustained.

AO2 It can be argued that an 'uncaused cause', even if it exists, is not necessarily the same thing as a theistic God. If so, it can be argued that the medieval view makes sense without God. On the other hand, it can be argued that Aquinas and others deliberately set out to integrate religious and philosophical ideas – and thus to provide an overall explanation of the universe that satisfied both religion and philosophy.

Further questions

1 To what extent might it be argued that science is based on a fascination with the world, and religion on a fascination with what lies beyond it? Answer with reference to the views of the world presented by philosophy and religion prior to the rise of modern science.

2 Why might a medieval thinker not have trusted the evidence of his or her senses?

3 THE RISE OF SCIENCE

Chapter checklist

In this chapter we shall look at key figures in the rise of modern science and at religious responses to their ideas. This will introduce some major issues that have caused problems for the religion–science interface.

Key words

Nihilism: the view that the universe is without purpose, but is simply the outworking of mechanical laws that operate under whatever conditions prevail at the time but do not have any 'aim' as such.

Deism: the view that the world was created by God, who established the principles under which it should operate, but does not interfere directly in its operation.

Heliocentric: describes a view which places the Sun (rather than the Earth) at the centre of the cosmos.

Empiricism: the view that all knowledge originates in sense experience.

Modern science has its origins in ideas that developed between the sixteenth and eighteenth centuries. Naturally, there have been hugely important scientific developments since that time – the theory of evolution, relativity, quantum mechanics, computing, neuroscience and so on – but in those centuries there developed a way of working with ideas and evidence, of conducting experiments and evaluating results, that established what we still see as the distinctive features of science.

The people who developed these ideas were often religious, and their conclusions did not necessarily conflict with religious ideas, but the general feature of this rise of science was the assumption that human reason, unaided by any divine or supernatural influence, was capable of understanding aspects of the way the world works. This threatened both the authority of religion and also the sense, particularly in some Protestant circles, that human reason was 'fallen' and therefore incapable of establishing the truth.

By the end of the eighteenth century, David Hume was able to argue about the right use of evidence and the origins of morality, and to criticise religious beliefs from a rational and atheist standpoint. While at the same time, William Paley, using the very image of human ingenuity and technology, was arguing for an understanding of God as designer – using the very success of human technology as a way of illustrating the part God might play in the world.

But we shall start this brief survey with two figures, whose observations contradicted conventional religious ideas and whose controversy therefore set the tone for later confrontations between science and traditional and dogmatic aspects of religion.

1 Astronomy

Key thought

Should theories be based on observation and experiment, or on the authority of Aristotle's philosophy and the teachings of the Church? That question was at the heart of some early debates between science and religion.

Key people

Copernicus (1473–1543) was a Polish priest and an astronomer. He did not consider that his science was in conflict with the teachings of his religion, but was cautious about making claims that appeared to contradict the medieval world view.

Key thoughts

The preface to Copernicus' work clearly recognises that religious authority might feel threatened by the development of new theories based on observation and reason, rather than on an unquestioning acceptance of the authority of ancient thinkers. Unfortunately (from our point of view) but prudently (from Copernicus' point of view), it merely side-steps the issue, rather than confronting it.

Although Copernicus appeared to challenge tradition with his heliocentric view of the world, he remained very Aristotelian in his thought. Asked why, if the Earth revolved, things did not fly off, he replied that evil effects could not follow from a natural movement. Asked why there was no constant wind because of the Earth's motion, he replied that the atmosphere, because it contained 'earthiness' (one of the four elements), revolved in sympathy with the Earth itself. These are Aristotelian answers. Later (as we shall see) Newton would have explained such things through gravity and the laws of motion, but Copernicus had not made the move into that sort of thinking.

The problems that were to face the interface between science and religion are well illustrated by the astronomy of the sixteenth and seventeenth centuries, for it was in the observation of the structure of the universe that clashes with the deductive arguments of the earlier medieval philosophy were most obvious.

In his main work on the movement of the heavenly bodies, *De Revolutionibus Orbium*, Copernicus claimed:

1 that the Sun was at the centre of the universe
2 that the Earth rotated every day and revolved around the Sun once a year.

This seemed to dethrone the Earth from its position in the centre of the universe, making it difficult to see why humanity should have cosmic significance. Copernicus also noted that there was no stella parallax (i.e. no shift in the relative position of the stars when viewed from two different places on Earth) and therefore correctly estimated that the stars must be considerably further away from the Earth than was the Sun. Clearly, such findings conflicted with the cosmology of Ptolemy, which had become an integral part of the Christian view of the universe.

When his book was published, a preface by the Lutheran theologian Osiander suggested that Copernicus was merely offering a more convenient and useful way of thinking about the universe, without claiming that his cosmology represented the way things *actually* were. (In other words: 'We know, through divine revelation, that the world is actually like X, but it might be useful, to help with our calculations, to think of it as like Y.')

However, two principles were established by Copernicus' work, which are important for understanding religion and science issues:

1 He established that scientific theories should be formulated on the basis of carefully gathered evidence.
2 His work implied that ideas established by the ancient Greeks, and which had become incorporated into Christian religious thinking, might actually be wrong.

This last point is most important. Christian teaching had identified itself with Aristotle's thinking, such that any challenge to that philosophy was regarded as a challenge to itself. Defending Christianity and defending Aristotle became linked in a way that brought Christianity into unnecessary conflict with the emerging sciences.

Other astronomers encountered similar problems.

Key word

Epicycle: an epicycle is the path traced out by a point on the circumference of one circle as it rolls around a larger circle. Copernicus and others used an elaborate system of epicycles to explain planetary motion.

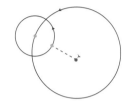

From the perspective of an observer in the centre of the large circle, the point on the circumference of the smaller circle does not appear to move in a circular orbit. However, it is actually moving in a circle around the circumference of another circle, the centre of which is itself moving around the large circle. Two perfect trajectories thus give the impression of a single imperfect one.

Key thought

Bruno illustrates the danger of using science as a basis for religious speculation. It was no more acceptable to the religious authorities then than theories based solely on religious ideas would be accepted within the scientific community today. That does not mean that Bruno was wrong – merely that he was unwise in the way he presented his ideas.

Key people

Galileo (1564–1642)
Regarded by Einstein as 'the father of modern physics', Galileo demonstrated that the forces of nature work in a regular, mathematical way. He also observed four moons orbiting Jupiter, thus controversially making a total of eleven heavenly bodies rather than the traditional seven. His book *The Message from the Stars* was published in 1610.

In 1572, Brahe (1546–1601) observed a new star. This may not seem remarkable today, but remember that, from the medieval perspective, all above the Moon was perfect and unchanging. He had therefore observed what the prevailing theory said could not happen.

Kepler (1571–1630) used both observation and mathematics to formulate the laws of planetary motion. He found a time difference between what he observed and what he calculated should be the case. The conclusion he came to was that the orbit of the planet Mars was not circular at all, but elliptical, with the Sun at one focus of that ellipse. This was a radical break with Aristotelian thought. Aristotle accepted the idea that perfect motion was circular: therefore the heavenly bodies must move in circles. Earlier astronomers, including Copernicus, had made their observations of non-circular orbits conform to Aristotle, by saying that the orbits were in fact **epicycles**.

Bruno (1548–1600) moved a stage further in challenging religious authority with speculative ideas based on the new cosmology. He read Copernicus in the 1580s and came to the conclusion that, since the Earth went round the Sun, the distinction between earthly and heavenly no longer applied. He declared that the universe could be infinite, and that there might be innumerable inhabited planets like ours. He then moved on to religious speculations based on such a cosmology, claiming that there could be many other incarnations and redemptions for those living on other planets. Such views clearly ran counter to Christian teaching and the Church responded forcefully; Giordano Bruno was tortured to death in 1600.

The developments in astronomy that had been taking place since the time of Copernicus came to a head, as far as the religion and science debate is concerned, with the work of Galileo, who believed that the Earth moved round the Sun, and was a heavenly body like any other.

In 1616, the Holy Office declared that it was 'revealed truth' (i.e. found in the scriptures) that the Sun moved round the Earth, and Galileo's view was therefore condemned.

In 1632, Galileo went on to publish his *Dialogue of the Two Chief World Systems* in which he compared Copernicus' view with the traditional one based on those of Aristotle and Ptolemy. He came to the conclusion that Copernicus was right, and moreover claimed that Copernicus had described the actual universe and had not simply offered a useful alternative way of making calculations (which is the guise under which Copernicus himself had put forward his ideas).

Galileo was put on trial and forced to recant. His trial marks a very negative turning point in the relationship between religion and science, and a breakdown of the medieval synthesis. He was condemned because he challenged the literal interpretation of scripture, and the authority of the Catholic Church. In its place he

Key thought

There is a certain irony in looking back at this debate between Galileo and the Inquisition. Galileo said that the Sun was fixed and that the Earth moved. The Inquisition said that the Earth was fixed and the Sun moved. That was the principal difference between them. From the standpoint of relativity, however, Galileo was (strictly speaking) no more correct than the Inquisition. The Sun and the Earth move relative to one another. Which moves round the other is simply a matter of perspective. The crucial difference was that *Galileo was prepared to consider a perspective that did not place humankind at the centre of things*.

had set reason and observation. To do so appeared to eliminate from science any place for providence or spiritual influence.

But Galileo had established two important scientific principles:

- that change comes about through *efficient* rather than *final* causality (to use Aristotle's terminology). Objects do not change because they seek a goal that lies in the future, but because they are acted on by previously existing forces.
- that the universe can be explained in terms of mathematical principles.

This did not mean that Galileo was not religious. His own view (which was put forward also by Francis Bacon) was that God had provided two different but complementary ways of looking at the world and understanding God: one through scripture and the other through nature. Those who condemned him would not allow the second of these to contradict a literal interpretation of the first.

2 Francis Bacon

Key people

Francis Bacon (1561–1626)
Opposed to Aristotle's idea of final causes, and determined to base all knowledge on evidence, Bacon anticipated the work of many later philosophers of science, and was also involved in the founding of the Royal Society. He is particularly known for *The Advancement of Learning* (1605).

Key thoughts

Bacon anticipated the twentieth-century argument about 'falsification' as presented by Karl Popper (see pages 38–39). To test the truth of a claim, one must seek out possible contradictions.

Francis Bacon should not be confused with Roger Bacon, who taught in Oxford during the flowering of science and culture in the thirteenth century, although they shared similar views on the place of reason and experiment – views which were at the forefront of progressive thinking in the early seventeenth century, but were quite astounding for someone writing 350 years earlier.

Aristotle had argued that knowledge is based on experience, but he had also argued that everything had a 'final cause' or purpose that defined its essence. The danger for science in Aristotle's thinking is that too much emphasis might be placed on trying to understand the final cause, at the expense of the basic work of observation and categorisation. Bacon was very aware of this, and he recognised that, in gathering evidence, there were a number of 'idols' which could tend to lead a person astray. These included:

- the wish to accept evidence that confirms what we already believe to be true
- distortions that result from our habitual ways of thinking (we see what we expect to see)
- muddles that come through our use of language (e.g. using the same word for different things, and then assuming that the things described must be one and the same)
- believing things because of one's allegiance to a particular school of thought.

Hence, Bacon argued that, in gathering evidence, one should not just seek those examples that confirm a particular theory, but should actively seek out and accept the force of contrary examples. At a time when science was expected to conform to the established beliefs of religion (as Galileo, Bruno and others discovered), this was a bold claim.

However, if you read Bacon expecting to find secular science devoid of, or opposed to, any idea of God, you are in for a surprise.

His work is shot through with references to God and to the scriptures. Clearly, knowledge gained through reason and evidence may not be compatible with superstition or the unthinking acceptance of authority, but Bacon certainly regarded it as compatible with a broadly religious outlook.

3 Newton

Key people

Sir Isaac Newton (1642–1727)
The title of his most important work *Philosophiae Naturalis Principia Mathematica (The Mathematical Principles of Natural Philosophy)*, published in 1687, says it all; Newton developed a natural philosophy (in other words, science) along mathematical principles. He set out the laws of motion and, famously because of an apple, recognised the nature of gravity. He established the principles of mechanics and optics and developed calculus. It is difficult to over-estimate his importance in the development of science.

Newton devised a system of physical laws which explained planetary motion, refining concepts such as mass, force, velocity and acceleration. He claimed that everything would either remain at rest or continue in its motion in a straight line, unless acted upon by forces. Therefore the world moved and changed according to fixed laws and, once started, would continue to do so without further external influence. Thus – to put it crudely – he presented the image of the world as a mechanism, which, once set in motion, would continue to move in ways that were predictable and reflected its construction.

This overall approach – which was hugely influential and successful, dominating science for almost 200 years – had two enormous implications for religion:

- Aristotle thought that divine spirits impelled things to seek their natural purpose or end. This was the cause of movement, without which everything would remain at rest. Newton had provided an alternative explanation for movement. What is more, he saw motion on Earth and in the heavens as fundamentally the same (whereas in the medieval scheme of things they were quite different, the latter being perfect and circular).
- Although the idea of God might be useful for explaining how the world started, God was not needed to explain its continuing existence and motion, since all was a natural working out of previous causes, following mathematical principles. Mathematics could predict motion.

Newton himself was religious, and he used an argument from design – namely that God lay behind, designed and guaranteed the mechanistic world. The world may work on mathematical principles, but God had provided those principles. Newton was also not above occasionally making reference to God in order to explain unusual phenomena – thus he invoked divine influence to explain variations from the predicted in planetary motion.

Newton's science was welcomed by many religious people because it was rational, and served to counter superstition and what was then called 'enthusiasm'. He was used as a basis for a 'natural religion' – based on deism and the idea that a rational universe had

Key thought

Of course, once God is removed from active involvement in the world, and is identified simply with the author of its rational and predictable physical laws and structures, it is only one further step to accept those structures but deny that they had a divine designer. What was seen by some as making God rational, others saw as making him optional!

been created by a rational God. In other words, rather than believe in a God who might selectively intervene in the world, Newtonian science offered the prospect of a world which itself displayed reason and order, as a sign of its divine creator.

The mechanical world of Newtonian physics was, however, a strange and rather dull place, reducing the richness of human experience to sets of mechanical and mathematical relationships. The twentieth-century philosopher A. N. Whitehead, commenting on the implications of seventeenth-century science, said:

> *Thus nature gets credit for what should in truth be reserved for ourselves: the rose for its scent; the nightingale for its song; and the sun for its radiance. The poets are entirely mistaken. They should address their lyrics to themselves, and should turn them into odes of self-congratulation on the excellency of the human mind. Nature is a dull affair, soundless, scentless, colourless; merely the hurrying of material, endlessly, meaninglessly.*

> *However you disguise it, this is the practical outcome of the characteristic scientific philosophy which closed the seventeenth century.*
> (*Science and the Modern World*, 1925)

This has enormous implications for such issues as freedom and determinism, miracles, design, or anything which concerns a religious or personal interpretation of experience. The perception of the world that took shape during the seventeenth century, and which was exemplified in the physics of Newton, was fundamentally materialist and mechanistic. It was a world formed out of the concepts (mass, location and energy) that scientists has abstracted from their overall experience.

Key thought

I may play a CD whose music moves me to tears, and yet – from the perspective of a narrowly defined science based on primary qualities (see pages 34–35) – I am told that what is 'real' is not the music at all, but the sequence of digital information on the disc. But that is not the whole story for, as Richard Dawkins points out in *Unweaving the Rainbow*, there is a sense of wonder that comes with appreciating the complexity of what is analysed. It is not that the digits are real and the music is not, rather that the wonder of science is in seeing the way in which the digits can and do transmit and reproduce what we experience as beautiful music.

But these abstractions, which summarised the dull, endless hurrying of material, were successful in predicting behaviour of material bodies, and thus could be used in science and technology. The crucial thing to recognise, from the standpoint of the history of the interaction between science and religion, is that *they were mistaken for reality*. The abstract notion of sound waves came to be seen as more 'real' than the music they described. In the popular mind, inspired by science, the universe became *identified with* this impersonal, mathematically predictable mechanism that scientists had abstracted from their experience.

The problem is that, once you have a world in which everything from atoms to stars is blindly following its patterned course, obeying impersonal laws, the more complex organisms (including human beings) start to be regarded in the same way. I can have no freedom or purpose in anything I do, simply because, in the mechanistic universe, every action is already fixed and determined.

In the nineteenth century, this view influenced ethical thinkers like J. S. Mill, who saw people's wishes and motives in terms of the conditions that brought them about. In other words, the *experience* of freedom had no place in the analysis of what led someone to act in a particular way; what really counted were the background causes and influences. We shall return to this issue of freedom and determinism in Chapter 8. For now, it is important to recognise that its origin lies in the way in which the scientists and philosophers of the seventeenth and eighteenth centuries identified abstract ideas with reality itself.

4 Practical science

Key thought

Eighteenth-century technology included:

- the steam engine (1712)
- the diving bell (1717)
- ball bearings (1749)
- the sextant (1757)
- Harrison's portable timekeeper (1759)
- the first balloon flight (1783)
- the steam boat (1783)
- gas lighting (1786)
- vaccination (1796)
- the parachute (1797)
- the electric battery (1800).

In terms of popular perception, these things acted as proof that science, based on observation and reason, must be right because it was able to deliver such practical benefits.

The seventeenth and eighteenth centuries also saw tremendous changes both in technology and in people's attitudes to reason and science. Defoe's *Robinson Crusoe*, published in 1719, presents the castaway as a man who survives through his own inventiveness. The new idea of that era was that nature could be understood and tamed through reason and technology. New instruments were devised – the air pump, telescope, microscope, barometer. *The Royal Society* in England and the *Academie des Sciences* in France were founded in the seventeenth century, and gave impetus to the emerging sciences.

The emergence of new technology was the most visible sign of the tremendous shift in self-understanding between the medieval world and people in the eighteenth century. The world was no longer a place dominated by spiritual forces, influenced by the planetary spheres, with a spiritual end in view. Rather it was a predictable, rational place, a giant mechanism, established by a creator God who did not need to interfere in its workings. This was very much the age of reason, with science as proof of its success.

5 Mathematics and statistics

Mathematics provided the background to much of the advancement of science in the seventeenth and eighteenth centuries. It is important to recognise the nature of mathematics and the very radical abstraction that it involves.

To put it crudely, you see one person, then another, then another, and as a result you say that there are 'three' people. The concept 'three' is an abstraction from your experience. There is no part of the colour, sound, sight, etc. that corresponds to 'three'. Having thus abstracted out from experience the concept of number, those concepts can be manipulated for all sorts of useful purposes. Mathematics, and science based on it, is essentially a way of

Key thought

If you say that sound is a set of vibrations in the air, you are abstracting from the experience of sound certain regular patterns that can be quantified and given numerical values, e.g. a musical note becomes a frequency that can be given a particular numerical value.

examining and manipulating these abstract concepts. What Galileo, Descartes or Newton were producing were formulae: ways of predicting; ways of calculating.

Hence 'laws of nature' or 'multiplication' are not *things* that exist; they are descriptions of the relationships between abstract concepts that human beings use in order to try to make sense of their experience.

To take a modern example, Stephen Hawking, author of *A Brief History of Time*, is interested in what happened in the very earliest moments of the universe, and does so by examining what happens in the phenomena known as 'black holes'. But he does not need to use a telescope for these investigations; rather he uses mathematics, and is, of course, a professor of mathematics. Science, and an understanding of the universe, depends heavily on the manipulation of concepts – and that is where mathematics plays such a central role. Developments in science may be possible as a result of developments in mathematics.

The nineteenth century saw another major development in the way in which science works – the use of statistics.

Today we take it for granted that scientists will present their findings in terms of statistical information. If we want to know whether particular activities (such as smoking or taking exercise) make a difference to a person's life expectancy we examine statistics that show the figures for those who do and those who don't smoke or take exercise.

Key thought

The link between lung cancer and smoking is not discredited on the grounds that a certain number of people are going to smoke and remain healthy. Statistics give only degrees of probability. They show a tendency, and that tendency is itself evidence for a physical cause, even if that cause cannot be proved directly. Indeed, statistics can suggest causal connections that then lead to research to pinpoint just why and how those causes operate.

The sociologist Durkheim (see page 123) analysed trends in human behaviour that could be measured, and concluded that there were social 'laws' at work that could be known statistically, even if they could not be measured directly. It was never assumed that statistics could prove what would happen to any one individual, but it was argued that, in looking at sufficiently large numbers, behaviour could be mapped and predicted. Statistics became a tool of scientific analysis.

6 The end of religion?

During the eighteenth century, both in Britain and on the Continent, philosophy developed in a way that reflected a new appreciation of the place of reason in human life. This new movement is generally referred to as the *Enlightenment*.

One example of this new spirit is found in David Hume (1711–76), the Scottish philosopher particularly known for his empiricism (the view that all knowledge starts with sense experience). His arguments about miracles (see pages 112–13) and his challenge to even the most cherished of religious concepts at that time – the idea of God as the designer of the universe – illustrate the intellectual freedom to challenge tradition in the name of reason and evidence.

Key quote

I have no need of that hypothesis.
LAPLACE, ON BEING ASKED HOW GOD
INFLUENCED THE MOVEMENT OF THE
PLANETS, WHOSE ORBITS HE HAD
BEEN RE-CALCULATING

Key thought

The move towards deism.
The new, rational view of the
universe developing at this time
allowed for an external, designer
God, evidenced by both the fact
of the world's existence and the
intricacies of its design. Such a
God, however, was not expected
to interact with the world, in the
sense of being personally involved,
or setting aside the 'laws of
nature' in order to produce
miracles. In particular, belief in
such a God did not involve
superstition or belief in what is
generally termed the
'supernatural' – it was seen as
compatible with science and
supported by reason and evidence.
The term for this belief is 'deism'.

Key thought

So you find that there were two
very different developments in
religious thinking in response to
the changed intellectual
environment:

- the move towards deism, and
  away from any form of
  religious superstition
- the move to separate religion
  from science and philosophy
  and to locate it in the sphere
  of the personal and emotional.

On the other hand, during the time of the rise of science, a majority of thinkers and scientists – including Copernicus, Galileo, Newton, Bacon and even Laplace – still claimed to hold religious beliefs that were not in conflict with their science. One way of expressing that was to say that the 'two books' of nature and scripture should be seen as separate but complementary. Reading Francis Bacon, one is struck by the systematic and careful way in which he looks at evidence and notes potential pitfalls in assessing it, while at the same time constantly quoting the Bible and referring to the world as God's creation.

However, during the seventeenth century there was a fundamental shift in attitude away from the idea that God might be revealed in the irregularities of nature – the miracles and the mysterious – to a sense that a creation that was not regular, mechanically sound and working with mathematical precision was not worthy of a divine creator. This led to emphasis on rational religion, devoid of superstition (as set out, for example, in Toland's *Christianity Not Mysterious*, 1696), to deism (the belief in an external creator God who is not personally or actively involved in his creation) and to the popularity of Newton's argument from design.

In contrast to deism, some religious groups concentrated on the personal and emotional aspects of religion, and were therefore unconcerned about the new mechanistic views of the universe. These included the Methodists in England and the Pietists in Germany. For them, religion and science were separate spheres of life, and they saw no need to argue from one to the other.

Some scientists and philosophers took the view that religion would be replaced by science – and they were encouraged in this by the very positive view of the future offered by the range of new benefits offered by technology.

By the end of the nineteenth century, Ernst Haeckel mocked the idea of a God as 'a gaseous vertebrate' (in other words, an impossibility), while celebrating the massive advances of science that had taken place by the end of the nineteenth century. In *The Riddle of the Universe* (1899), he celebrated the triumphs of science over superstition by taking a materialist view of the universe, in which every aspect of life develops from its material matrix. Since Haeckel's position is one that appears incompatible with freedom as well as with most traditional religious beliefs, an outline of his argument in given in Chapter 8. He represents one extreme of the nineteenth-century debate, utterly opposed to the Romantics' reaction against what they saw as science's excessive drive to rationalise experience and formulate abstract theories.

Key people

Ernst Haeckel (1834–1919)

was a naturalist and biologist, concerned with mapping out the tree of life, and known for his theory that the development of each individual recapitulates the evolutionary process by which its species has evolved. His main philosophical contribution was written in German between 1895 and 1899 and published in English as *The Riddle of the Universe* in 1901.

James George Frazer (1854–1941)

Frazer's massive work, *The Golden Bough*, published in 1922, was subtitled *A Study in Magic and Religion* and represented a major attempt on the part of an anthropologist to understand how ancient religious practices and superstitions might relate to Christianity and to religious beliefs in general.

Cross-reference

See Chapter 4, section 6, for more on logical positivism.

Other thinkers, taking religion more seriously, still saw it as a limited phase in humankind's self-understanding. Frazer (author of *The Golden Bough*, a huge exploration of religion and culture) saw three stages in human development:

1 magic – through which people try to manipulate nature
2 religion – belief in supernatural powers that rule the world
3 science – leading to human self-reliance, based on observation.

As humanity develops, therefore, religion is likely to diminish. Many came to assume that the scientific method was the only way to gain true knowledge.

These things, taken together, represented a general growth in the view that science could offer (in theory, if not in practice) an overall explanation of the world, without reference to the idea of God. Meanwhile 'God' was relegated to the subjective feelings of believers, or the projected aspirations of society.

What is clear is that, by the end of the nineteenth century, there was a feeling – encouraged by the debate over evolution – that religion had, for many thinking people, been replaced by science. It was a view that, early in the twentieth century, was to influence the philosophers of the logical positivist movement, who saw the success of science as a model for establishing criteria by which they could decide which statements were meaningful and which meaningless. And, of course, the criterion they took was that the meaning of a statement was given in its method of verification. In other words, all meaningful language should be backed by empirical evidence, and without that, language (including most religious language) was meaningless.

The vision of a science-led quest for truth that would embrace and take over the functions previously performed by religion is elegantly (if rather one-sidedly) expressed by Haeckel:

> *The goddess of truth dwells in the temple of nature, in the green woods, on the blue sea, and on the snowy summits of the hills – not in the gloom of the cloister, nor in the narrow prisons of our gaol-like schools, nor in the clouds of incense of the Christian Churches. The paths which lead to the noble divinity of truth and knowledge are the loving study of nature and its laws, the observation of the infinitely great star-world with the aid of the telescope, and the infinitely tiny cell-world with the aid of the microscope – not senseless ceremonies and unthinking prayers, not alms and Peter's pence. The rich gifts which the goddess of truth bestows on us are the noble fruits of the tree of knowledge and the inestimable treasure of a clear, unified view of the world – not belief in supernatural miracles and the illusion of an eternal life.*

> (*The Riddle of the Universe*, 1899)

In updated form and with less flowery language, this could almost be attributed to Richard Dawkins. The retreat from the original integrity of the philosophical and scientific quest with a religious viewpoint, which was there in Aquinas or Newton, has given way to a polarisation of the enthusiasm for the open quest for knowledge, contrasted with a reactionary retreat into religion whose beliefs are based on revelation and authority.

And yet Haeckel – as much as Dawkins more than a century later – presents the wonder of scientific discovery in terms that go a long way to address the need for awe and wonder, for direction and the quest for truth, that for many people have been expressed in terms of religion.

Summary diagram

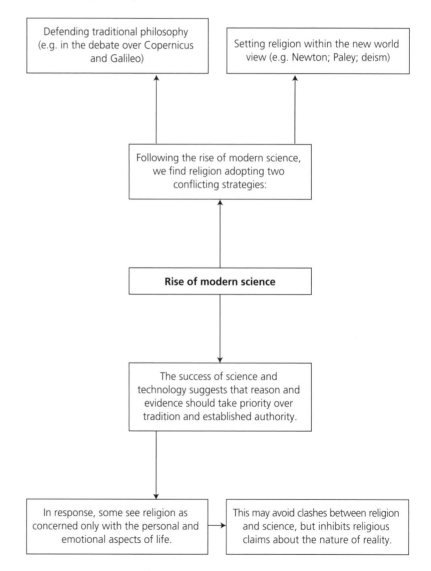

Study guide

By the end of this chapter you should appreciate the challenges posed to religion by the rise of modern science, and appreciate the different approaches taken to reconcile these two aspects of life.

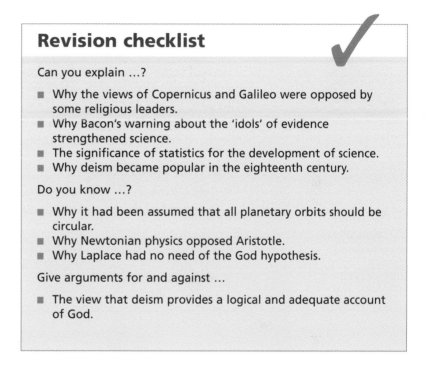

Revision checklist

Can you explain ...?

■ Why the views of Copernicus and Galileo were opposed by some religious leaders.
■ Why Bacon's warning about the 'idols' of evidence strengthened science.
■ The significance of statistics for the development of science.
■ Why deism became popular in the eighteenth century.

Do you know ...?

■ Why it had been assumed that all planetary orbits should be circular.
■ Why Newtonian physics opposed Aristotle.
■ Why Laplace had no need of the God hypothesis.

Give arguments for and against ...

■ The view that deism provides a logical and adequate account of God.

Examples of essay questions

1. The seventeenth and eighteenth centuries saw the triumph of reason over superstition. Do you agree? Give your reasons.

AO1 This would require a broad awareness of the basis of science in reason and evidence, and of the claim that religion was based on superstition. It should also include the fact that religion depended upon the earlier philosophy of Aristotle, so it could be justified rationally, and the 'deist' approach to religious belief – allowing it to be compatible with the developing sciences.

AO2 This could involve a consideration of the extent to which religion claimed to be rational, and an appreciation that most scientists in this period would have considered themselves to be religious.

2. To what extent does the history of the debate between religion and science endorse Frazer's view that there is a development from magic, through religion and towards science?

AO1 This could include a survey of the development of philosophy – showing that religion may be based on a rational interpretation of the world, and therefore parallel to science. It would also be relevant to show ways in which religion facilitated and encouraged science. It would also be relevant to discuss whether science, through its derived technologies, provides the sort of control of the environment that magic (and/or religion) might once have claimed to give.

AO2 It would be appropriate to consider whether science has replaced religion in terms of a satisfying overall view.

Further questions

1 Critically assess the impact of science upon the Christian religion in the seventeenth and eighteenth centuries.

2 Is it possible for religion to be totally devoid of mystery? Assess this with reference to issues concerning the relationship between religion and science.

4 METHOD, LANGUAGE AND AUTHORITY

Chapter checklist

In this chapter we shall look at the method used in scientific enquiry, the language used to convey its findings, and the way in which the authority of scientific theories is established.

Historically, the foundation of the modern scientific method required three things:

1 a trust in evidence and experiment as means of acquiring knowledge
2 a desire to challenge and evaluate all claims to truth, setting aside the authority of both the Church and Aristotle
3 a belief that the world is both orderly and intelligible.

There is no reason, in principle, why these should bring science into conflict with religion, because:

● The evidence of the senses had always been taken into consideration by religion, as Aquinas and other theologians had shown in presenting arguments for the existence of God.
● The authority of the Church had already been challenged at the Reformation – showing that human reason and the ability to study and discuss ideas in scripture did not destroy but rather enlivened religion.
● The traditional cosmological argument for the existence of God was a classic example of linking religious belief with the conviction of orderliness in the universe.

The only real challenge was that the emerging scientific method was organised, self-contained and – above all – successful!

But there was another issue raised by the success of science: the scope and function of language. By the early years of the twentieth century, there were those who argued that, unless a statement could be backed up by evidence, it was meaningless. In other words, all meaningful statements should conform to the norms of science. This challenged the meaningfulness of both religious and ethical language and raised broader questions about what such language was doing.

1 Evidence and sense experience

Cross-reference

For further information on Descartes, his rationalist approach to the theory of knowledge, and his use of radical doubt, see Chapter 3 of *The Theory of Knowledge*, in this series.

Key words

Rationalism: the view that all knowledge starts with the processes of human thought.
Empiricism: the view that all knowledge starts with sense experience.

Key people

René Descartes (1596–1650)
Descartes questioned the reliability of sense experience, and concluded that the only thing he could not doubt was the actual fact of his thinking – hence his famous claim 'I think therefore I am'. Descartes embarked on this quest for certainty because he wanted to place Catholic belief on firm rational grounds in order to counter the scepticism of his day.

Key question

How do you relate the primary qualities (number, size, shape, duration) to the secondary qualities (colour, sound, smell, touch) in the way human beings experience their world?

Francis Bacon, Newton and others had insisted that knowledge started with observation, from which reason could deduce the laws of nature, expressing them in mathematical terms. This claim that all knowledge comes from experience is termed **empiricism**.

By contrast, Descartes, often described as the founder of modern philosophy, used the method of systematic doubt in order to establish what could be known for certain. Since the senses can sometimes deceive us (e.g. when mistaking a dream for reality) he doubted all empirical evidence. His only certain knowledge was of himself as a thinking being ('I think therefore I am'), since to deny it would involve self-contradiction. This approach, seeing the mind, rather than the senses, as the starting point for knowledge, is termed **rationalism**.

Generally speaking, the method that has dominated the world of science since the seventeenth century has been based on empiricism rather than rationalism. In other words, it has started with observation and experiment rather than with pure thought. However, this general claim needs to be qualified, since it is clear that our understanding of the world depends upon the way in which we interpret the information that comes through the senses – our own mental processes and perceptions have a part to play; no evidence is free from interpretation.

Primary and secondary qualities

The philosopher John Locke took an empiricist view of the theory of knowledge; in other words, he believed that everything we know comes from sense experience. But he recognised that there was a difference between perceiving shape, for example, and colour. He therefore divided the qualities ascribed to an object into two categories: primary and secondary. The distinction was clear:

- Primary qualities belonged to the object itself, and did not vary according to the way in which it was perceived, e.g. something had a particular mass and was in a particular location.
- Secondary qualities depended upon the faculties of the person perceiving them, or the circumstances in which they were perceived.

Key people

John Locke (1632–1704)
Locke, famously claiming that the human mind started off as a *tabula rasa*, a blank slate, waiting to be written on by experience, became the first major empiricist philosopher. His great work on the theory of knowledge is his *Essay Concerning Human Understanding* (1690).

Key thought

All we can know and comment on are the regularities in what we experience. Everything continues to be dependent upon our methods of perception and measurement. We cannot get absolute facts about the world as it is, only the world as we experience it.

Key people

Ernst Mach (1838–1916)
Mach worked as an experimental physicist. He took the view that scientific laws were the summary of experimental evidence and therefore reflected the ability and need of the mind to systematise complex data, rather than corresponding directly with the external world. He pointed to the unique nature of all real events – events only appear as identical in terms of our summary descriptions of them.

Cross-reference

An outline of logical positivism is given in Chapter 5 of *An Introduction to Philosophy and Ethics*, and for the issues of perception and interpretation see Chapter 8 of *The Theory of Knowledge*. For Wittgenstein, see below, page 47.

Thus, for example, colour, smell and sound depend upon our faculties. As the light changes, or if it grows dark, the colours we see will also change; the phenomenon of colour says something about our perception, not about a quality that can be fixed and ascribed to an object.

Science therefore attempted to reduce everything to primary qualities that could be measured, and which seemed to be objective and fixed – nature as 'a dull affair, soundless, scentless, colourless; merely the hurrying of material' as Whitehead commented (see above, page 25).

Let us look for a moment at the implication this has for the scientific view of the world. Light is analysed into waves or particles; sound into vibrations, or changes in air pressure. Our experience of the sound, as something beautiful, or being at a particular pitch, was no longer seen as the 'real' description. Sound was *really* just a set of vibrations, only becoming what we experience as sound through the working of our ears.

As a result of this emphasis on primary qualities, it was commonly argued in the early part of the nineteenth century that science was able to give a complete explanation of things by way of mechanical laws inherent in things themselves, and that there was no longer any place for superstition or personal views in the interpretation of natural events.

However, it was soon recognised that, when we examine experience, it is the *phenomena* of our experience that we are dealing with, not the things out there in the world as they are *in themselves*. Hence science is about the *mental interpretation* of the structures of the world – you cannot leave the thinking and observing subject out of account.

This was the view taken by Ernst Mach, in his *The Analysis of Sensations* (1886). He saw science reflecting on facts that are the contents of consciousness given by sensation, and therefore they should all be reduced to statements about sensation, rather than claiming that they could refer directly to the external world. From Mach's point of view, scientific theories were just accounts of phenomenal regularities – i.e. they summed up what had been experienced.

And this whole tradition led towards the work of Bertrand Russell, Wittgenstein and the logical positivists, who saw meaningful statements as summaries of experience, and as verifiable only with reference to experience.

Hence, in looking at experience, we see a shift from the assumption that it is possible to speak of external facts, to the awareness of the interpretative and mental nature of what is experienced. We will need to keep this shift in mind as we look at the basics of the scientific method.

2 The scientific method

Key quote

… it is not what a man of science believes that distinguishes him, but how and why he believes it. His beliefs are tentative, not dogmatic; they are based on evidence, not on authority or intuition.

BERTRAND RUSSELL, *THE HISTORY OF WESTERN PHILOSOPHY*

Key word

Methodological naturalism: the view that scientific enquiries are limited to observations of this world, and therefore that they cannot deal with the 'supernatural' except in so far as it has a natural component or effect.

'Method' refers to the process by which beliefs are established, and the grounds upon which they may be defended. Clearly, the exact way this is done varies from one branch of science, but it is important to be clear about the general principles involved.

The inductive method

There are two fundamentally different processes involved in gaining knowledge: deduction and induction.

The deductive approach

If you know one mathematical equation, you can deduce others from it; if you know the rules by which a game is played, you can deduce what individual moves are likely to be made. There is nothing wrong with the inductive method as such: provided that you know that the rules are correct and that they apply to this particular situation, various things can be deduced that are perfectly valid. You do not have to conduct experiments to know that 2 + 2 = 4 in each and every case; it is known to be true by definition.

Sometimes, however, what is deduced does not square with what is experienced – we do not see what reason tells us we should see. In such cases, we need to look at the assumptions upon which the deduction is based. So, for example, the medieval view of the heavens was that they were perfect, and therefore that the planets had to move in circles, since the circle was a perfect shape. This piece of deduction conflicted with evidence, and therefore the underlying assumption (the perfection of the heavens) was challenged.

The inductive approach

The inductive method, which was the key feature of the development of science, works in this way:

- Observe and gather data (evidence; information), seeking to eliminate, as far as possible, all irrelevant factors.
- Analyse your data, and draw conclusions from it in the form of hypotheses.
- Devise experiments to test out those hypotheses, i.e. if this hypothesis is correct, then certain experimental results should be anticipated.
- Modify your hypothesis, if necessary, in the light of the experiments.
- From the experiments, the data and the hypotheses, argue for a theory (this is the crucial stage in the inductive part of scientific method).

- Once you have a theory, you can – using deduction – predict things that should be the case if your theory is correct.
- Establish tests which can either verify or disprove the theory.

It is clear that this process of induction, by which a theory is arrived at by the analysis and testing out of observed data, can yield at most only a *high degree of probability*. There is always the chance that an additional piece of information will show that the original hypothesis is wrong, or that it only applies within a limited field. The hypothesis, and the scientific theory that comes from it, is therefore open to modification.

Theories that are tested out in this way lead to the framing of scientific laws. Now it is important to establish exactly what is meant by 'law' in this case. *In science, a 'law' simply describes behaviour; it does not control it.* If something behaves differently, it is not to be blamed for going against a law of nature; it is simply that either:

- there is an unknown factor that has influenced this particular situation and therefore modified what was expected, or
- the law of nature is inadequately framed, and needs to be modified in order to take this new situation into account.

Generally speaking, an activity is called 'scientific' if it follows the inductive method. On these grounds, the work of Marx could be called scientific in that he based his theories on accounts of political changes in the societies he studied. Similarly, a behavioural psychologist can claim to be scientific on the basis of the methods used – observing and recording the responses of people and animals to particular stimuli, for example.

In evaluating what counts as science, method counts for more than subject matter. Thus, for example, astronomy is regarded as a science; astrology is not. This is because the former is based on observable facts, whilst the latter is based on a mythological scheme. This is important in setting boundaries around what can be considered to be true science, but it does not necessarily follow that science within those boundaries offers the *only* route to true knowledge – that is the claim of **scientism**.

What is clear from the above is that science is naturalistic – in other words, it deals with the natural world as it is experienced. This does not necessarily mean that the only entities that exist are those that can be encountered in this way, but it provides a practical limitation to scientific method. That method is based on observation, and is therefore concerned with the natural, physical world. The term used for this is 'methodological naturalism'.

Key thoughts

In common parlance, 'law' is taken to be something which is imposed, a rule that should be obeyed. But that is not the case in science. A scientific law is a systematic way of describing what has been experienced – it describes; it does not command.

Empirical evidence leads to the development of theories. But we often find that the same evidence could be equally well explained by two or more theories. The problem is then how you decide between (or if you need to decide between) these theories. This feature of the relationship between data and theories is termed 'empirical under-determination'.

Key word

Scientism: the term 'scientism' is generally used for the view that science *alone* can give true knowledge of reality, and it alone can determine what is meaningful. Such an approach tends to ignore the contribution of the arts to human self-understanding. Sadly, in many debates, scientism is presented as though it were science. So, for example, Richard Dawkins, who excels in presenting the wonder of science, falls into the language of scientism when attacking his caricature of religion, thereby undermining his own argument.

3 Logic and progress

Key questions

How does the challenging and modifying of theories enable science to progress?
How can you ensure that your interpretation of the evidence you gather is not distorted by assumptions based on existing theories?

Key thought

If 'God exists' is taken as a scientific hypothesis, it should be possible to specify exactly what observations should count for and against it. If it is claimed that the existence of God is compatible with all logically possible evidence, then that claim is not scientific.

Key people

Karl Popper (1902–94)
Born in Vienna, Popper encountered the logical positivism of the Vienna Circle of philosophers, but rejected their positivist view that language could only be meaningful if backed *positively* by empirical evidence. In its place he argued that a claim could be meaningful if it could be specified what evidence might *falsify* it. He became interested in political issues, and was critical of both Marx and Freud, claiming that neither allowed their theories to be open to falsification. His major works are *Logic of Scientific Discovery*, 1934 (but not published in English translation until 1959), and *The Open Society and its Enemies*, 1945.

Karl Popper, in his book *The Logic of Scientific Discovery* (1934, trans. 1959), makes the important point that science seeks theories that are both logically self-consistent, and that can be *falsified*. It is curious to think of science as a process by which existing theories are falsified, but that is the implication of Popper's view. The reason lies in the method by which that theory has been reached in the first place.

A scientific theory goes beyond what can be experienced. It takes all the available evidence, and on the basis of that frames a general hypothesis – a hypothesis which should, if it is correct, account for other situations for which we do not have evidence at present. Now, it is possible to go on collecting more and more data to illustrate the truth of the theory. The more evidence we have, the more likely it is that the theory is correct. We can never absolutely *prove* that a theory is true by this method – all we can show is that it continues to account for the evidence.

Science makes progress, however, once a theory is shown to be false or in need of modification. In other words, a scientist comes up against evidence that does not fit the theory, and consequently the theory has to be modified in order to take the new evidence into account. A scientific theory is therefore accepted on a provisional basis until such time as it is falsified.

This leads Popper to say that a scientific theory *cannot be compatible with all the logically possible evidence. If a theory claims that it can never be falsified, then it is not scientific.* For science it is important to have statements that contain real information; but the more information it has, the more likely it is to be proved incorrect. This is its strength, not its weakness, for if you find a statement with the maximum probability of being true, it will contain minimal information. For example, I may say 'The sun will rise tomorrow'. This has a maximum probability of being true, but it will hardly cause any excitement, nor revolutionise people's views. On the other hand, if I say 'It will start raining at 6.47a.m. tomorrow', that information might be quite important, but has a high probability of being false – and is certainly not going to be true for all locations! *The ideal for science is to be able to make statements with the maximum amount of information that is compatible with a real possibility of that information being correct.*

At one time, science's attempt to maintain objectivity and ensure that all evidence was theory free would have been presented as the principal difference between the scientific and the religious methods. Yet things no longer seem quite that simple.

Key thoughts

Popper pointed out that no observations are free from the interpretation placed on them by the observer. We also tend to be selective in what evidence we consider to be relevant. Hence the process of induction is never as simple or as foolproof as it might appear. But that is not to deny that observation and experiment provide the best available method of discovering facts about the physical world.

For Popper, scientific theories are 'instruments of thought'; in effect they are highly informed guesses about what will happen in the future, based on what has been observed in the past. They can therefore be falsified (if things fail to happen as predicted) but never absolutely verified.

First of all, it is increasingly recognised that objectivity in science is far from easy. The way in which data is collected and the criteria by which it is analysed and presented are both bound up with existing theories. On the other hand, the personal view of a particular scientist should not influence the acceptance or rejection of evidence, or of a theory arising from it. Equally, the overthrow of a previously influential theory is not regarded as a failure, but as a success — since it means that a new theory can emerge that takes even more evidence into account.

By contrast, religion is concerned with personal views, and religion offers a framework of beliefs with which to interpret experience. But that does not prevent religions from making claims about the nature of the universe. Indeed, if a religion makes no factual claims, it could be regarded as simply one way of looking at things, with no reason to prefer it over any other — and that would hardly satisfy religious believers. But, of course, once factual claims are made, they may be assessed on exactly the same basis as any other factual statement, tested out against evidence and so on.

Example

We shall look at miracles in Chapter 9. But consider what religion means by a miracle in the light of this discussion of objectivity. If the account of a 'miracle' makes factual claims of an unusual sort, these can be checked by criteria other than those of the religion itself (in other words, there can be an attempt at objectivity). On the other hand, if by 'miracle' is meant no more than a particular way of viewing an event, there is no reason to challenge its validity, for no factual claims are being made. A traditional 'miracle' (e.g. a unique event that appears to violate an established law of nature) tends to claim high factual content (i.e. it makes claims about specific facts) with correspondingly low probability. Something with low factual content (i.e. it claims the obvious, or few checkable facts) and high probability (e.g. that the sun will rise tomorrow) is hardly going to be regarded as a miracle.

4 Models and paradigms

Key words

Model: an image, taken from common experience, used in order to explain a phenomenon.
Paradigm: an example of established scientific work, used as the basis for further developments in the subject.

Key thought

Models can be 'adequate' if they are a practical help to us in understanding reality, but they cannot be 'true' because we cannot observe reality directly and make a comparison.

Scientific **models** are analogies drawn between something familiar and the object of scientific investigation, in order to help people visualise or understand conceptually what is being studied. These models may need to be revised as the scientific view changes and the original analogy no longer holds.

For example, until the nineteenth century, the atom was thought of as a small ball of matter, solid and indivisible. In the early twentieth century, that model was no longer adequate, and was replaced by the model that saw the atom as a miniature solar system, with electrons circling round a nucleus like planets round a star.

In the same way, at any one time, the results of scientific work in the past are used as a basis for present research. That is quite inevitable, for otherwise everyone would have to start from scratch every time. These examples of past work, along with their methodologies and concepts, are termed 'paradigms'. A **paradigm** is a general way of looking at a situation, and it tends to survive minor changes in the models that surround it.

Every now and then, however, science makes a radical leap forward, in what may be termed a paradigm shift. When that happens, data is re-evaluated in the light of the new paradigm. Otherwise, most scientific work is a routine matter of filling in information within an already existing paradigm. The theory of paradigms was developed by S. Kuhn in his influential book *The Structure of Scientific Revolutions* (second edition, 1970).

A fundamental disagreement about how science makes progress may be illustrated by the views of Popper on the one hand and Kuhn on the other. Popper's view was always radical, with every theory being open to be falsified at any time. By contrast, Kuhn's was more conservative – based on the observed fact that, for most scientists for most of the time, they get on within the parameters of established theories, working on details and improvements, rather than being open to a wholesale discarding and re-building of theories. For Kuhn that established pattern of thinking forms a 'paradigm'. A 'paradigm shift' only happens when the existing paradigm theories are convincingly shown to be failing, and an entirely different way of looking at things presents itself. For most of the time, however, the authority of the scientific community as a whole is what determines what is acceptable.

Key thought

CHALLENGES AND PROGRESS

If a scientist comes up with a theory that is completely different from all that has gone before, it may represent progress, or it may simply be a false alley down which mainstream science should not venture. Einstein challenged and shattered Newtonian physics, showing it to be of limited application, but that is not regarded as a failure for science, rather a step forward. Kuhn's approach tends to be cautious in this respect, since most will carry on working within the existing paradigm, until the weight of contrary evidence becomes overwhelming.

However, just because something contradicts the established view – e.g. the idea of intelligent design, challenging Darwin's view that the appearance of design is the result of natural selection over a long period of time – does not mean that it should be dismissed. It is required of science that a serious consideration needs to be given to every approach, and ideas should only be discarded if they can be shown to be contrary to the overwhelming bulk of evidence, or not in line with a rational interpretation of that evidence.

In other words, reason and evidence should provide sufficient authority for the acceptance of a theory, and therefore we should be prepared to set aside any theory if decisive evidence goes against it.

5 Certainty and authority

Key question

If the religious quest requires certainty, does that mean that religion should cease to make any factual claims that may be challenged on the basis of evidence?

We have seen that making a scientific statement involves an element of risk; if it has any positive content and value, there will always be a chance that it will be proved false. But human beings, faced with a world full of risks, may long for religion to provide them with certainty, in the form of authoritative statements about the world, God and so on.

Key questions

- Should science (as an activity) be influenced by the authority of the established scientific community?

And a parallel question ...

- Should religion (as an activity) be influenced by the established religious communities?

One answer to both of these is to say that individuals will probably want to be guided by the experience of a majority of those engaged in the same activity, but that individuals may sometimes take a step (whether scientific or religious) that takes them beyond what has been done or understood before.

a) Certainty and proof

We have seen that, from a scientific point of view, proof is obtained by the best available interpretation of evidence available. A hypothesis is put forward and is tested out. The proof that something is the case is thus never fixed in an absolute sense – it is a proof based on our present knowledge, always open to the possibility of future revision. Nevertheless, to say that something has been proved to be the case implies that there is adequate evidence to convince a rational person of the truth of a statement. If there is scientific proof for something, it would require new evidence, or a clear indication of a misinterpretation of the existing evidence, for that proof to fail.

As we saw in the last section, there is debate within the scientific community about just how far particular theories may continue to be used once challenged by experimental results that challenge them. Kuhn took a fairly conservative view, holding on to theories until they were clearly no longer viable. Popper insisted that all theories should be open to falsification, and others have suggested that it is perfectly acceptable to allow a range of different theories to compete with each other, to see which is best at giving an explanation – ruling no theories out of court just because they are not regarded as mainstream in scientific terms.

It is this openness to the possibility that a theory may eventually be proved wrong, or inadequate, that sets the authority of scientific claims apart from those of religion, and leads some people to complain that religion is being based on 'blind faith' rather than reason and evidence. But is that necessarily the case?

It is clear that religion cannot offer absolute proof. Arguments for the existence of God, for example, are open to a variety of interpretations. It is always possible that they will need to be revised.

Key thought

From a scientific point of view, there is no absolute certainty when it comes to theories. Revision is always a possibility. In this sense, a scientist is likely to say 'I am convinced by the evidence that "X" is the case'. Or 'I consider "X" to be the best explanation'. But not simply 'I am committed to the belief that "X" is true'.

Key thought

FAITH OR BLIND FAITH?

Some critics tend to label any religious view as one of 'blind faith'. This implies that something is believed (in the sense that it is believed 'that' it is the case, rather than believing 'in' something, which simply expresses personal commitment) irrespective of all evidence. In other words, it implies that the believer is blind to reason and evidence.

Some religious believers may indeed take that position, but others would argue that faith need not be blind, but can be the conclusion of a process that includes (even if it is not limited to) the normal process of examining evidence and coming to a balanced conclusion. Those taking such a position may indeed be open to the possibility that they are wrong, just as a scientist will be open to having his or her theories modified or replaced as new evidence emerges.

In evaluating science and religion issues, it is important not to assume that all believers are alike in this respect.

Key quote

Blind commitment to a theory is not an intellectual virtue: it is an intellectual crime.

IMRE LAKATOS

Key thought

Karl Popper argued that the aim of science was not simply to provide statements with the maximum probability of truth, but to produce statements with real, informative content. And the more specific the content, the more open it will be to the possibility that it is wrong.

Some astrologers produce statements that are so general they can apply to anyone. They may not be proved wrong, but they don't give any helpful factual advice either.

Therefore, the more religious claims are specific and factual, the more they are open to be proved wrong.

Key people

Søren Kierkegaard (1813–55)
Kierkegaard argued that an impersonal approach to understanding the world did not do justice to the responsibility and inward experience of the individual in making decisions about matters of belief and behaviour. He emphasised the responsibility and challenge of individual choice in shaping people's lives, particularly in the areas of religion, morality and self-understanding, thus initiating the existential approach to philosophy. His books include *Either/Or* (1843), *Fear and Trembling* and *Philosophical Fragments*.

But in the case of religion, a believer may feel 'absolutely certain' of, for example, the existence of God. This certainty is not merely an interpretation of facts, but is born of personal conviction. To be certain of something implies that you place your trust in it, that you are committed to it. It is to be relied upon, and not open to doubt.

Is it possible to be certain of something for which there is no proof? You can say, for example, that you are certain that a particular person will arrive on time. You do this on the basis of previous knowledge of that person's behaviour, or his or her general reliability. But clearly there is no way that you can offer proof that he or she will turn up on this particular occasion.

Of course, previous experience is also the basis of scientific proof. The more consistent observations of a particular event are, the more likely it will happen again in the future. In this sense, your certainty about a person's behaviour is built up in the same way that a scientific hypothesis is built up. On the other hand, once you say that you feel certain, you have taken a step beyond issues of evidence and the balance of probability; you are committed. A good scientist will therefore only say that something appears certain 'on the basis of present evidence' – always leaving open the possibility that new evidence might challenge his or her view.

In the Prayer Book service for the burial of the dead, the clergyman speaks of the 'sure and certain hope of the resurrection from the dead'. This does not imply *proof* of the resurrection, simply a commitment (based, for example, on the belief that evidence for Jesus' resurrection is correct) to hope that it is so. It is expressed as a hope that is 'sure'; in other words, it is based on evidence and beliefs of which that person feels certain.

b) An existential approach

Kierkegaard was concerned to show that faith was not a matter of logical conclusions, but of making a personal commitment. It was the intensity of one's personal choice that defined faith. This reflected the earlier Lutheran position and has characterised much Protestant Christianity. It places personal commitment at the centre of faith, and thus as directly opposed to the process of rational evaluation that characterises the scientific method.

Feelings and attitudes, although described as 'subjective', are a vital part of our experience of the world. William James put it like this:

> *To describe the world with all the various feelings of the individual pinch of destiny, all the various spiritual attitudes, left out of the description … would be something like offering a printed bill of fare as the equivalent of a solid meal.*

(*The Varieties of Religious Experience*, 1902)

We saw (above, pages 34–35) how the distinction between primary and secondary qualities seemed to deprive the world of Newtonian physics of all those things that made it rich and beautiful. But we have also seen (as in Richard Dawkins' *Unweaving the Rainbow*) that there can be a sense of beauty, wonder and poetry in the scientific view of the world. Facts and scientific analysis do not eliminate the sense of wonder.

It is therefore important to distinguish carefully between commitment and emotion or wonder. You can have the latter without the former. You can have a view that includes emotions and aesthetic appreciation, without clinging on to a particular interpretation of that experience. By contrast, commitment is – by definition – something not easily shaken. It implies a determination to maintain a particular view, even in the face of evidence to the contrary.

Key thought

In science, it is recognised that observations are often 'theory laden'. In other words, our observations are not free from the perspectives that come from the theories that we already hold. The same is true for religion. Those who believe in miracles, or that good can come out of suffering, will interpret what they experience in the light of those beliefs. For religion, far more than for science, *experience is not neutral between theories, but is coloured by them.*

Example

The clearest example of religious commitment to a view concerns the problem of evil. Suffering and evil are evidence against the hypothesis that there is an all-loving and all-powerful God. But the religious believer does not see this as a reason to abandon his or her belief, but tries to re-interpret the evidence, hoping to find some alternative explanation for it that gives an overall good outcome. In other words, once committed to belief in the existence of God, evidence is either made to fit, ignored, or the whole matter regarded as a mystery. It is precisely this sort of commitment that goes against the methods used by science.

At its heart, science represents the view that all claims to factual knowledge should be assessed in terms of reason and evidence. Those claims that are not backed up by evidence are suspect, and are liable to be challenged. That applies equally to claims made on the basis of science and those made on the basis of religious faith. If a factual claim is made by a scientist, it is put forward in such a way that its basis in reason and evidence is set out and open for scrutiny. If the factual claim is made on the basis of religious authority, or personal experience, it should equally be open to scrutiny. *Factual* claims can be checked against the evidence. If they are not substantiated, that does not automatically mean that they are wrong – there may be evidence forthcoming that we have not yet encountered – but they will be held as (at most) tentative hypotheses. If a more plausible one – i.e. one better evidenced – comes to light, that will be preferred.

The problem is that, because of the nature of religious commitment and authority, it is very difficult for a religious believer to accept that religious truth claims can be open to that degree of scrutiny and possible refinement or replacement.

So where should the authority for factual claims lie, with reason and evidence, or with religious experience or commonly accepted religious doctrine?

c) Sources of authority

Reason and revelation

Some theologians – especially Thomas Aquinas – have argued that faith in based on both reason and revelation. Through natural law, something of God's nature can be known through reason, but that knowledge is supplemented by divine revelation.

By contrast, Luther and other Reformation theologians argued that humankind's reason was subject to the 'Fall' and was therefore incapable of knowing God. If everything that the unaided reason can achieve is futile, faith must be based on revelation and commitment and, if not contrary to reason, at least independent of it.

Those who take this view will say that the scientific is in principle incapable of either proving or disproving religious truths.

Experience and community

A religious experience has authority for the person who has it. It may give him or her a new perspective on life which colours, or is used to interpret, all that happens. Similarly, a religious organisation, in framing doctrines and moral principles, exerts an authority over its individual members – stemming from the respect that the individual has for the whole body of experience and insight upon which that religion is founded. Religious beliefs therefore depend on authority and are not adopted or changed simply on the basis of reason.

By contrast scientific enquiry seems to accept no authority other than the commitment to deal rationally with evidence that is presented in an experiment. When we look at the history of science, however, we see that authority plays a part, and that theories only become established once accepted by the scientific community as a whole.

If a scientist comes to a conclusion that is at odds with the views of a majority of his or her colleagues, it may be very difficult to get the results of that scientific work accepted. For example, scientific journals may be unwilling to publish it. From time to time there is a 'paradigm shift', when the scientific community accepts a very different way of looking at a phenomenon. Before that happens, however, there will be scientists who have to go against accepted scientific principles in order to get the new views established. Thus, science moves forward as theories become widely accepted by the scientific community.

Key thought

Science starts with a problem, devises hypotheses to solve it, tests them out and accepts what works.
  Buddhism starts with the problem of suffering and the need for happiness, suggests ways in which suffering can be overcome and invites people to test these out and accept only what works.

Key quote

At the heart of Buddhism and in particular at the heart of the Great Vehicle (the Mahayana), great importance is placed on analytical reasoning. This view holds that we should not accept any teaching of the Buddhas if we were to find any flaw or inconsistency in the reasoning of that teaching. It is advisable, therefore, to adopt a sceptical attitude and retain a critical mind, even with regard to the Buddha's own words. Does he himself not say, in the following verse, 'O Bhikshu, as gold is tested by rubbing, cutting, and melting, accept my word only on analysis and not simply out of respect.'

THE DALAI LAMA, *BEYOND DOGMA*

A similar process takes place within religion. Views about the nature of miracles, for example, may gradually come to change. Thus, at the time when Hume was writing, he probably reflected the view of a majority of religious people when he referred to a miracle as a violation of a law of nature. Today, many religious people would not want to take that point of view, or would qualify it considerably (see Chapter 9, section 2).

It is therefore inaccurate to suggest that science is based on reason while religion is based on authority: both make claims that depend to some extent on both reason and authority. The essential difference, however, is that the scientific method accepts that every claim may be challenged, in the light of new evidence.

This contrast tends to be made in the context of Western theistic religion, but may not apply to all religions. In the case of Buddhism, people are encouraged to examine and try out its teachings, and to accept them only to the extent that they are personally convinced of their truth.

Rationalism and empiricism had placed human reason, based on observation, at the heart of the new way of understanding the world. It had produced results, and was defended as a new enlightened way of seeing things – contrasted by the superstition of earlier eras.

We have also seen – particularly in the case of astronomy – that the new scientific method of gathering data and forming hypotheses came into direct conflict with the authority, both of ancient philosophy (particularly Aristotle) but also of the Church.

The Church claimed to speak with authority and to give people certainty. Science too seemed to offer certainty, backed up by reason. This built on the new-found intellectual challenge brought about by the Reformation and then the Enlightenment – reason and religion challenged each other in terms of which would offer certainty and which could speak with authority.

Social acceptability

Sometimes a scientist will say something that is not acceptable socially or politically. Thus, for example, James Watson – famed for his work in discovering the structure of DNA – appeared to claim that there was a difference in the intelligence of people of different races, while visiting London in 2008 to launch a new book. His remarks gave offence and he was severely criticised, the Science Museum cancelled his lecture, and he returned to America, where his employers had suspended him from his post of Chancellor of Cold Spring Harbor Laboratory. The Mayor of London said 'Such views are not welcome in a city like London' and one journalist described him as a 'racist nut' and 'elderly loon'.

Whether or not Watson meant what he said, and quite apart from any scientific discussion as to whether there could be difference in intelligence between different racial groups within *Homo sapiens*, this raises again the issue of authority.

At the time of Copernicus and Galileo, radical views were over-ruled by authorities on the grounds that they challenged deeply held beliefs. The same is true today. A scientist – even one otherwise held in great respect – is expected to conform to socially acceptable norms. In this case, it is moral and social views about racial equality, rather than about religious views, but the principle remains the same.

On the other hand, those who try to use science in order to back up their independently held views (e.g. that the world is young and was created in seven days) are criticised from within the scientific community, either for basing arguments on prior beliefs, rather than on reason and evidence, or for selecting evidence to suit their beliefs.

Hence the issue of scientific method and authority is not simple. Acceptance of scientific theories is still dependent upon social acceptability.

6 The issue of language

Key quote

The limits of my language mean the limits of my world.
WITTGENSTEIN, *TRACTATUS*, 5.6

Key people

Ludwig Wittgenstein (1898–1951)
Trained in engineering and fascinated by mathematics and logic, Wittgenstein's early work (*Tractatus*) examined the limits of knowledge, linking it closely with what could be verified by experience. His work inspired the Vienna Circle of philosophers, and the approach to language known as logical positivism. Later, he broadened his view of what counted as a meaningful statement, taking into account the different ways in which language is used.

At the beginning of the twentieth century some philosophers, impressed with the obvious success of the scientific method, sought to analyse language and to show where its meaning could be verified with reference to the sort of evidence that would be appropriate for science. To know if a statement is correct, it is only necessary to check it against the empirical facts upon which it is based. Thus the early work of Wittgenstein, followed by that of Schlick and others in the Vienna Circle – later to be popularised by A. J. Ayer in *Language, Truth and Logic* – argued for what is generally known as logical positivism, namely that the meaning of a statement is its method of verification. Hence, if I were to say 'There is a cat under the table' it means 'If you look under the table you will see a cat'.

In his book *Tractatus Logico Philosophicus*, Wittgenstein took the view that the function of language was one of picturing the world and thus started with the bold statement:

The world is everything that is the case. (*Tractatus*, 1)

and equates what can be said with what science can show:

The totality of true propositions is the whole of natural science. (*Tractatus*, 4.11)

Key thought

Wittgenstein was profoundly influenced by William James, especially his work on mysticism. This may account for the references to mysticism at the end of *Tractatus*. He accepts that the most important things cannot be said – not the view of a cynic, but of a follower of James.

Key word

Mysticism: the intuitive sense of going beyond the limitations of space and time, and feeling at one with, or at home in, the universe.

Key question

We know that clouds, being formed of water droplets, cannot experience loneliness, nor do they wander. We also know that daffodils, being organic, are not made of gold. Should we therefore ban the teaching of Wordsworth in schools?

It ends however with the admission that when it comes to the mystical (the intuitive sense of the world as a whole) language fails; we must remain silent. What is 'seen' in a moment of mystical awareness cannot be 'pictured'. It cannot be expressed literally. He ends with:

> *Whereof we cannot speak, thereof we must remain silent.* (*Tractatus*, 7)

Any statement for which there was no empirical evidence that counted for or against its truth was deemed by the logical positivists to be either a tautology, or meaningless. On this basis, logical positivism considered that most religion was meaningless.

From the middle of the twentieth century, however, this view generally gave way to a broader one in which it was recognised that different forms of language functioned in different ways. For example, if I should say 'Stop!', what I am saying is not meaningless, but it is not a description of anything. I am simply using language to bring something about. Following the later work of Wittgenstein and others, it came to be recognised that different forms of language each have their part to play, and their meaning is given in terms of the form of life within which they operate. Hence religious language was no longer branded as meaningless simply because it did not conform to a norm set by science.

Religious language is misused if it pretends to be scientific. For example, the 'God-of-the-gaps' problem (see pages 75–76) arose because language about God was being used in place of a scientific explanation to fill the gaps in existing knowledge.

But the recognition of the variety of forms of language, and its relationship to the circle of people that use it, is crucial also for understanding the way in which scriptures should be interpreted.

A crude, logical positivist approach would suggest that individual claims in the scriptures should be taken literally and checked against the relevant evidence. That evidence can show the claim to be either true, false or meaningless.

Decoding the Bible

An advertisement appeared in the *Guardian* in August 2002 placed by 'The Lord's Witnesses' and claiming that 'We now have good evidence that we have fully decoded Revelation 13 and 17 (in the first symbolism)'.

Apart from the rather worrying claim that the present system of things ends in 2008, it also noted that it had been

Key thoughts

To recognise the subtle beauty of a poem is not to go soft on its literal significance, but to show its true meaning and purpose!

Some people are desperate for an authority that will overwhelmingly reassure and remove the pain of doubt. The danger of this lies with *radicalism*. A radical may take an aspect of political argument or an economic theory and apply it with ruthless determinism (as happened, for example, in Stalin's Russia). Equally, a radical may take a religious doctrine and defend it to the death – whether his or her own, or that of other people. In each case, a fixed idea becomes the ultimate source of authority, rather than the process of reason or intuition that originated it. Radicalism threatens religion and science equally, and is countered in both by an insistence on factual claims being backed up by reason and evidence, and non-factual (e.g. poetic, symbolic, mythological, personal) ones being recognised and valued for what they are.

prophesying since 1992 that the UN would become the pre-eminent world power in the seventh last year of this system, and that this had been shown to be correct because, through the International Criminal Court, it had authority over all military personnel since 1 July 2002. The 'seventh biblical king' (the UK–US world power) thus gave way to the 'eighth biblical king' (the UN).

Quite apart from questions about whether the United Nations has become the world power, or the extent to which the US and others accept the authority of the International Criminal Court, this highlights an extreme form of biblical interpretation. A document written 2000 years ago, using cryptic language to explore the religious and political events at a time when Christians were persecuted by the Roman authorities, is taken to be a secret code, giving information about events in the twenty-first century. Made popular by fiction, this sort of 'code-breaking' approach to ancient religious texts creates real problems for the religion and science debate, since it gives the impression that texts can be interpreted without reference to their original context and language. Such interpretation clearly goes against exactly the sort of systematic examination of evidence on which science is based.

A more sophisticated approach would look at the language used and would ask what the writer was intending to convey, whether the words should be taken literally, metaphorically or poetically.

Summary diagram

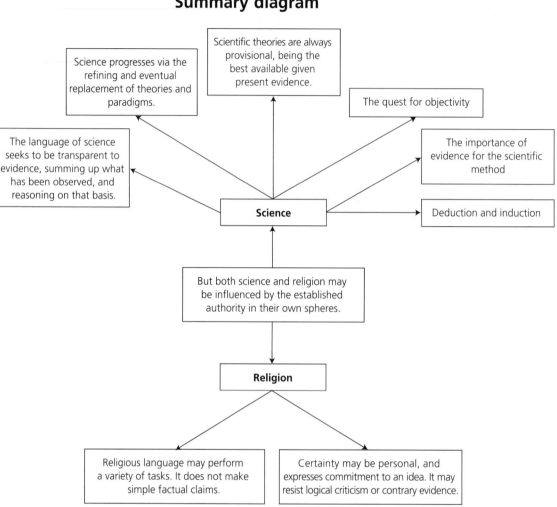

Study guide

By the end of this chapter you should appreciate the way in which scientific theories are produced, and how they may be refined and replaced. You should also understand the problem of taking religious claims as though they were scientific, and recognise the different nature and function of religious language.

Revision checklist ✓

Can you explain ...?

- Why a religious quest for certainty is incompatible with the provisional nature of scientific statements.
- How authority plays a part in both religious and scientific communities.

Do you know ...?

- The difference between deductive and inductive reasoning.
- Why the logical positivists argued that religious claims were meaningless.

Give arguments for and against ...

- The view that statements can only be trusted if they are based on reason and evidence.

Examples of essay questions

1. Discuss the view that science looks for proof, while religion looks for certainty.

AO1 This requires a basic knowledge of the scientific method, showing that proof is based on evidence and logic, and pointing out that such proof is always provisional and therefore never absolutely certain. There would need to be some appreciation of the existential element in religious commitment, and therefore of personal certainty.

AO2 In assessing this, one might point to the fact that – to make progress – science is always open to new ideas, but is certain only about its methods, not its results. Equally, there could be an exploration of the view that religion is about commitment, rather than certainty about any specific claims to truth – perhaps taking the view that the truths of religion are beyond literal description.

2. To what extent can it be argued that religion and science rely on completely different sources of knowledge?

AO1 As with the previous question, it is important to show a knowledge of scientific method. It can then be pointed out that the truth claims of religion cannot be supported by the same method, since they do not make straightforward factual claims. It is also important to point to scriptures and revelation as sources of knowledge for some religions.

AO2 In this assessment, it can be pointed out that traditionally religion has been based on philosophy (e.g. the traditional arguments) that claim to be based on reason and evidence, but that the existential need for a sense of meaning and purpose, which people may look for in religion, is beyond what can be given through empirical evidence.

Further questions

1 To what extent is Locke's distinction between primary and secondary qualities relevant to issues that may divide religion and science?

2 For religion, unlike science, certainty is possible but proof is impossible. Discuss.

5 MODERN PHYSICS AND THE NATURE OF REALITY

Chapter checklist ✓

Relativity and quantum mechanics have revolutionised physics, showing Newtonian physics to be correct only within certain very limited parameters. This chapter provides a brief introduction to each, and also considers the mystical and religious views of the nature of reality, to see whether they are compatible with modern physics.

1 Relativity

Key question

Is religion compatible with the world revealed by relativity and quantum mechanics?

Einstein formulated two theories of relativity. The first (in 1905) is termed 'special relativity'. This is summarised in the formula $E = mc^2$, linking mass and energy. Since E stands for energy, m for mass and c for the speed of light, the formula shows that a very small mass is equivalent to a very large amount of energy.

The second, termed 'general relativity', followed in 1916. It showed that time, space, mass and energy are all related to one another. Through the influence of gravity, both space and time may be changed. Thus, for example, time passes more slowly where there is less gravity, and space is also elastic, being compressed as gravity increases. But gravity is related to mass – since the larger the mass of a body, the greater its gravitational pull – and mass (according to special relativity) is related to energy.

There are two key things to appreciate about the significance of this for religion and science issues:

- Relativity encourages a 'holistic' approach to understanding the universe. Einstein's theories were a major step in the direction of finding a single theory to explain everything. Relativity shows that everything is interconnected.
- Relativity did *not* show Newtonian physics to be wrong; rather it showed that it described laws that operated *within a very localised and limited set of conditions.* If you consider space, time, gravity and

mass as they appear to an observer on the Earth's surface, then Newtonian physics works well. On the other hand, once you start to look at the extremes of the universe, gravity starts to warp both space and time, and the Newtonian perspective is of little use.

Since Einstein's day, great progress has been made in working towards 'theories of everything'; the goal of discovering the most fundamental principles that link all the basic forces in the universe, showing how they have developed and therefore exactly how they relate to one another. Relativity was the first step in the direction towards such an overall theory.

Relativity can assist in developing a more subtle view of the nature of 'God'. If the world were crudely mechanical, it might be possible to ask if there were a creator God *outside* it – and that was very much the view of the deists (see above, page 28). Relativity shows the inadequacy of any such view. Space, time, 'outside' and 'before' take on a very different meaning in this interconnected world, and one that does not allow any caricature of an external creator to be taken literally.

On the other hand, just as Aquinas' 'unmoved mover' points to but does not totally define the God of most believers, so it would be unwise for believers to assume that the discovery of the 'theory of everything' would provide a mathematical formula to explain God.

Key thought

The quest for a 'theory of everything' is not new. The pre-Socratic philosophers were looking for just that. Nor does it exclude the religious viewpoint; Aquinas' 'unmoved mover' was seen as the single idea that gave meaning and coherence to everything.

Key question

Could a mathematical formula – even one that unlocked the secrets of our universe – replace what people mean by 'God'?

2 Quantum mechanics

The idea that matter comprises atoms separated from one another by empty space is not new; it was a view put forward by the Greek atomist philosophers Leucippus and Democritus in the fifth century BCE (see above, pages 8–9).

However, a major new development came about early in the twentieth century with the recognition (following a discovery made by Max Planck in 1901) that radiation (e.g. light, or energy) did not seem to arrive as a continuous stream, but as little packets or 'quanta' – hence the term 'quantum theory'.

Until the discovery of the electron in 1897, the atom was thought to be indivisible, and was visualised as a very small but solid portion of physical matter. The atom was then found to have a nucleus comprising protons and neutrons, with electrons circling round it, like planets in a solar system. It was insubstantial; mostly empty space.

Particle physics (the term used for the study of sub-atomic particles) developed from that point, with atoms recognised as made up of many different particles, divisible into smaller 'quarks', which themselves come in different forms. Matter is therefore far from simple. It is composed of complex arrangements of nuclear forces, binding together particles, which themselves cannot always be distinguished as independent entities.

Aristotle had made a distinction between the material cause of something and its formal cause. We think of something having a particular form and made out of a substance.

> *But when we come to the ultimate particles constituting matter, there seems to be no point in thinking of them as consisting of some material. They are, as it were, pure shape, nothing but shape; what turns up again and again in successive observations is this shape, not an individual speck of material.*
>
> (E. Schrödinger, *Science and Humanism*, 1952)

Of course, shape here does not refer to geometric shape – particles are far too small to be thought of in that way. The shape here is the patterns that give evidence for that particle.

This is quite a difficult concept to grasp, but is essential to an understanding of modern physics. The pictures or models we use to describe things cannot be true or false (since we cannot compare the picture with the original to see if it fits); rather we can describe them as adequate or inadequate. A model is adequate if it can be used successfully in predictions.

Take the example of iron. When a small amount of iron is set within an electric arc, it heats up to a very high temperature, and the iron vapour gives off a distinctive spectrum of light (which shows up as tens of thousands of individual lines in the spectrum pattern). That spectrum pattern is always the same, wherever iron is found. Thus even if we cannot see iron atoms, we know if iron is present by observing the spectrum of light. Thus it is possible to tell what distant stars are made of, simply by analysing the spectral patterns of the light they emit.

Particles seem to change, depending upon how they are observed, and at this level their behaviour appears to be random (unlike the predictable laws of Newtonian physics). This leads to an important feature of quantum theory that is sometimes misunderstood and can cloud the associated religion and science issues. *Quantum theory cannot predict the action of individual particles, but describes the atomic world in terms of probabilities, based on the observation of very large numbers.*

There arose a debate between Niels Bohr, a quantum physicist who held that such uncertainty was inherent in nature, and Einstein, who rejected the idea of random happenings – declaring 'God does not play dice' (see below, Chapter 8, section 6), and arguing that indeterminacy was a feature of our measurement, rather than of reality itself.

Key thoughts

When a lump of iron is heated, it glows, but the light emitted at that temperature is continuous across the spectrum. This is because the individual iron atoms are close together, and interfere with one another, thus blurring the individual lines of the spectrum. It is only at extremely high temperatures that the distinctive lines emerge. *This is another example of the way in which things emerge in extreme conditions that would not have appeared in the conditions of our everyday experience.*

The uncertainty in Quantum Theory is rather like an opinion poll, which can predict how a population will vote, but is unable to be precise about the way in which any one person will do so.

Key thought

The debate between the Copenhagen interpretation of quantum mechanics (represented by Bohr and Heisenberg) and that of Einstein and Schrödinger centred on whether observation represented reality, or whether reality is prior to and is therefore independent of our observation.

A similar debate can be had about religious language and ideas. Are they simply a convenient way of describing a reality that is independent of them, or do these religious ideas create their own reality?

To put it bluntly, is the word 'God' a way of describing reality, or is God real?

In 1927, Heisenberg pointed out that, in an experiment, the more accurately the position of an atom is measured, the more difficult it is to predict its velocity (and *vice versa*). It is impossible to know both things at once. The crucial debate here – as highlighted by Einstein's original objection – is whether such uncertainty is caused by the way in which we examine nature, or whether it belongs to nature itself. In other words, is it just that we have not developed the right technique for the simultaneous measuring of the speed and position of an atom, or is it that the atom is not something of which it is theoretically possible to specify speed and position?

It also has implications for the freedom and determinism debate which we shall examine in Chapter 8. Laplace had argued that, in theory, everything in the universe can be predicted from a knowledge of the present: quantum theory denies this. However, it should be remembered that this indeterminacy applies only to this atomic and sub-atomic level of reality. The implication of quantum mechanics is that physical events, once they are down to the atomic or sub-atomic level, cannot be observed to have a cause. All that we have is a *probability* of causes – in the sense of a statistical likelihood of one thing rather than another being the case. Once we start to deal with larger objects, however, the principles of Newtonian physics still apply. Hence, it is unwise to cite Heisenberg as a scientific support for a theory which claims that, for example, the actions of human beings cannot, in theory, be predicted.

Key thought

SCHRÖDINGER'S CAT

Schrödinger proposed a thought experiment. A cat is placed in a box, along with a bottle of cyanide which will be smashed by a hammer if a decay in a radioactive substance is detected. We cannot tell whether the cat is alive or dead until the box is opened and we take a look. But what is the status of the cat prior to the box being opened? Common sense suggests that the cat must be either dead or alive, prior to the box being opened.

Consider the parallel with quantum mechanics. Bohr's approach would suggest that it is only the act of looking that determines reality (hence the cat is neither dead nor alive until we look) but Schrödinger wants to argue that reality exists one way or another prior to our observation. We cannot *know* whether the cat is dead or alive, but it must *actually* be one or the other.

Key thought

Once again, this is not a new debate. In ancient Greece, Protagoras argued that all we know are the sensations we receive, whilst Democritus argued for 'things' that existed independent of our sensations.

In all this, it also becomes clear that there is a totally new relationship between observer and observed. The world cannot be divided between independent, objective things and human observers. *Whatever we observe, we influence.* The quantum physicists Bohr and Heisenberg made this clear with the implication that an object has no existence independent of our observation of it. We cannot get 'outside' our process of observation to see what is 'really' there – it makes no sense to think in those terms.

3 The origins of matter

Key thoughts

Remember, most of the universe is empty space. Physical matter is a rare exception to nothingness. But even solid bodies are mostly empty space; tiny particles held together by hugely powerful forces that give the appearance of solidity.

The elusive Higgs Boson has sometimes been nicknamed 'the God particle'. Its discovery (or the discovery of its equivalent) will finally close the God-of-the-gaps argument – for the creation of matter out of pure energy is exactly the function that traditional belief has ascribed to God, and a physical explanation of that process will close off the final and most important gap. That, of course, does not close the religion and science debate at all; it simply shows the inadequacy of the God-of-the-gaps approach.

A key problem for science is why there is matter. We know that a small amount of matter, if broken apart, creates a huge amount of energy – based on Einstein's $E = mc^2$, that was the basis of the atomic bomb. We also know that in the first moments of the 'Big Bang' energy was converted into matter. But how? Why did matter and anti-matter not simply annihilate one another? Why were there ripples in the originally smooth early universe that led to the formation of the galaxies in the universe as we know it now?

One theory is that mass comprises particles that are somehow glued together. But by what? In 1964, Peter Higgs, a physicist working on this problem, suggested that there were tiny things called bosons, that had the effect of clustering and holding particles together to create mass. Hence the quest for what is called the 'Higgs Boson' – and possibly an explanation for why mass formed out of energy.

Scientists at Cern, located near Geneva in Switzerland, are currently working on an experiment that will recreate conditions similar to those of the 'Big Bang'. The Large Hadron Collider accelerates strings of particles around a circular tunnel, 25 km in circumference and 105 m below ground, until they are travelling at near the speed of light, and then crashes them into one another. They hope that, as a result, they will be able to detect the Higgs Boson, or whatever else it is that leads to the creation of physical mass.

Traditionally, while the way the universe works has been left to physics, the fact that there is a universe at all has been left to philosophy and theology. The quest for the particle that forms mass from energy appears at first sight to suggest that physics is on the verge of answering that question.

However, discovering the mechanism by which mass is created from energy is not the same thing as saying why there is anything at all, for one can simply push back one stage and ask why there is energy in the first place. Hence, without denying the advances that physics can make in this field, there is still scope for engaging in questions about the nature of the universe from a personal and religious point of view. The important thing is to recognise that physics and religion do not offer *alternative* explanations, but potentially complementary viewpoints on the same amazing phenomena.

4 Mystical and religious perceptions

Sadly, much of the dialogue between science and religion has been carried out by way of caricature. Scientists are presented as being insensitive and blind to deeper human emotional and aesthetic qualities – wanting everything proved and measured. Religious people are presented as wilfully naïve, clinging to a crude notion of God that science has long ago shown not to exist, and all too ready to threaten hellfire.

In fact, there is a real case to be made for saying that the scientific quest itself, and the wonders of the universe revealed by modern science, are profoundly religious. This does not imply that scientists secretly believe in God, even if they claim to be atheist, but that the motivation to understand the universe, and to celebrate the evolving complexity of living things, springs from a deep sense of wonder that is also at the heart of the world's religions.

When, in *The God Delusion*, Richard Dawkins set out to attack religion, he chose as his target a literal, fundamentalist view of God, and dismissed as irrelevant to his argument the religious views of Einstein. This is not surprising, because – from Einstein's point of view – Dawkins is a very religious man! His sense of wonder at the creativity of nature and the magnificence of the whole process of evolution are not far removed from the views of some religious mystics, and his campaigning zeal has all the hallmarks of evangelicalism. So let us explore the religious possibilities of modern science, taking Einstein himself as our starting point.

In an article for the *New York Times* magazine, 9 November 1930, Einstein poses the following question:

> *Feeling and longing are the motive force behind all human endeavour and human creation, in however exalted guise the latter may present themselves to us. Now what are the feelings and needs that have led us to religious thought and belief in the widest sense of the words?*

Key quote

I am a deeply religious nonbeliever.
ALBERT EINSTEIN, FROM A LETTER
DATED 30 MARCH 1964
(ARCHIVE: 38–434)

Key thought

Einstein argues that the deep convictions that a scientist has about the rationality of the universe, and the yearning to understand it, are fundamentally religious.

That does not re-define what a scientist feels or does; it simply defines what, in the broadest sense, is meant by religion.

His answer is that the motives are fear, but also the social impulses and moral ideas. But he adds another – a cosmic religious feeling 'which knows no dogma and no God conceived in man's image'.

For Einstein, religion is concerned with a mystical awareness of the nature of the world at large. In other words, he is looking at the mystical sense of meaning and wonder that goes beyond our normal perception of things in the world. He also makes a clear distinction between the areas of concern of science on the one hand and morality and religion on the other:

> For science can only ascertain what is, but not what should be, and outside of its domain value judgements of all kinds remain necessary. Religion, on the other hand, deals only with evaluation of human thought and action; it cannot justify speaking of facts and relationships between facts. According to this interpretation the well-known conflicts between religion and science in the past must all be ascribed to a misapplication of the situation which has been described.
>
> (*Science, Philosophy and Religion: A Symposium*, 1941)

But is he right in seeing the conflicts as being simply about misapplication, or are there genuine and logically unavoidable clashes between science and religious beliefs?

To answer this we need to return to the fundamental distinction between religion itself and religious beliefs. A person may have a sense of the wonder of nature and may call that religious, he or she may even call it an experience of God, but until that religious experience is encapsulated in a form of words – a proposition, such as 'there exists a God who created the world' – there is nothing with which science can disagree.

Equally, if the language used is recognised as poetic or analogical, there is no problem. No scientist is going to challenge Robbie Burns' claim that his love is like a red, red rose. We know that those words are used to hint at a particular emotion. The problem is that, if someone says 'I have experienced God', it may simply reflect a sense of wonder at the natural world, or a feeling of being forgiven, or of a vision of what one should do. But if it then becomes fossilised in the proposition 'God exists', it may be mistaken for a scientific claim about existence (much as one might argue for the existence of an electron) and therefore challenged.

But relativity and quantum mechanics have demonstrated that the world is a rather more flexible and surprising place than we might formerly have imagined. They endorse rather than diminish a sense of wonder. And that – shorn of its dogmatic propositions – is also where religion is coming from.

Key people

Fritjof Capra (b.1939)
Fritjof Capra, a physicist working in California, published *The Tao of Physics* in 1975, linking quantum mechanics to Eastern mysticism. His work broadened into looking at ecology, lifestyles, sustainability and so on – seeking to parallel developments in modern physics with religious insights, both Eastern and Western.

Key quote

Modern physics ... pictures matter not at all as passive and inert, but being in a continuous dancing and vibrating motion whose rhythmic patterns are determined by the molecular, atomic and nuclear structures. This is also the way in which the Eastern mystics see the material world. They all emphasise that the universe has to be grasped dynamically, as it moves, vibrates and dances; that nature is not a static but dynamic equilibrium.

FRITJOF CAPRA,
THE TAO OF PHYSICS, 1975

In *The Tao of Physics*, Capra argued that there were basic features of modern physics, and particularly quantum mechanics, that had parallels with Eastern mystical traditions. In particular, Capra saw the fundamental sense of the unity and interconnectedness of everything, which is at the heart of Eastern spirituality, as something to be explored and paralleled in modern physics. He noted also that, in Eastern mysticism, reality is dynamic rather than static – constantly on the move. Indeed, the foundation of Buddhist philosophy is the sense that everything is always in a state of change, and that the attempt to prevent this and cling to something fixed, whether an object or an idea, is the root cause of suffering.

As physics seemed to be moving away from a very static model of objects placed within empty space, to be replaced with the dynamic idea of waves, so it seemed to move nearer to Eastern spiritual intuitions. Indeed, sub-atomic particles do not make sense as isolated 'things' but only as connected with one another; hence the fact that they can be seen either as particles or as waves.

Interconnectivity through waves in space seemed to be a very appropriate way of describing the old problem for Eastern spirituality – how the individual was connected to the whole of which he or she felt intuitively to be identified. A wave moves across space, and within that wave, individual particles move and are connected with one another.

Other writers have taken this up and expressed a whole range of spiritual practices – meditation, healing and so on – in language that is clearly borrowed from quantum mechanics.

The fundamental question, however, is whether it is legitimate to take a language and set of concepts that make sense in one field of study and apply them to another. Thus, if you have a mystical intuition that everything in the universe is connected to everything else – a common feature in the experiences of those practising meditation, bringing with it a sense of warmth, connectedness and overall meaning to the world – does that necessarily relate to any quantum ideas about non-causal connections, or communication at greater than the speed of light? The same words might well take on very different meanings when used in such different contexts.

It is also clear that, whereas quantum mechanics has been very successful in practical terms, as a way of calculation, it is far more problematic when it comes to using it to explain fundamental features of reality.

But there is a yet more fundamental reason why quantum mechanics is unlikely to provide a scientific underpinning for a mystical vision. The standard interpretation of quantum mechanics is that taken by Bohr and Heisenberg (the Copenhagen interpretation). This claims that the indeterminacy is fundamental to the way in which we experience things – it is not simply a matter

Key thought

Quantum mechanics is enormously difficult to understand. Mostly it is counterintuitive – in other words, its explanations do not follow the normal rules of logic. That leaves it open to a wide range of interpretations. Clearly, some mystical intuitions are similarly beyond conventional explanation, and hence the temptation to set them alongside quantum mechanics – rather as deist ideas were set alongside the mechanical world of Newtonian physics. Whether, in the long run, religious ideas are well served by such an attempted parallel is quite another matter.

of asking whether the cat is dead or alive in its box (to use Schrödinger's thought experiment) before we take a look, because we do not have an independent awareness of reality with which to compare that which we experience. All we know is the experience – it is meaningless to ask if the cat is dead or alive, until we are able to take that look and we see which is the case.

This means that quantum mechanics, however useful it might be in aiding practical calculations, is about experienced reality. You cannot separate experience and reality.

But this is *also* the position of meditation and mysticism – what is experienced is the reality. One cannot get outside or beyond the mystical experience to obtain independent, scientific evidence to show that it is either right or wrong.

Hence the problem with trying to link quantum mechanics to mystical intuitions – they both tend to inhabit their own self-contained fields of understanding. Neither can really serve as an endorsement of the other.

Summary diagram

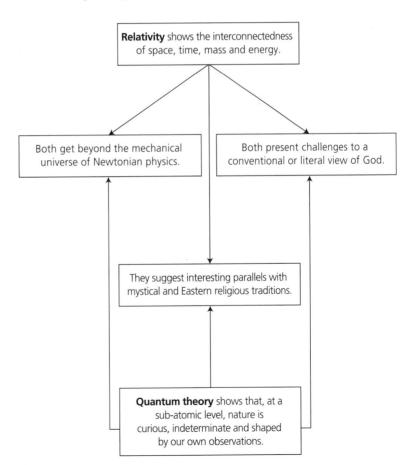

Study guide

By the end of this chapter you should have a broad understanding of those features of relativity and of quantum theory that are relevant for an appreciation of the way religion and science relate to one another, and have considered the implications they have for an understanding of the mystical approach and of ideas about God.

Revision checklist ✓

Can you explain ...?

- ■ How modern physics shows the limitations of Newton.
- ■ What is meant by indeterminacy at the sub-atomic level.

Do you know ...?

- ■ Why you can't know what happened to Schrödinger's cat.
- ■ Why a modern scientific view of the universe is more likely to appeal to religious mystics than the older Newtonian view.

Give arguments for and against ...

- ■ The view that an understanding of modern physics makes it easier to be religious.

Examples of essay questions

1. Relativity and quantum theory, by broadening the horizons of physics set by Newton, require a believer to take a correspondingly broader concept of God. Discuss.

AO1 This requires a brief outline of the way in which modern physics has shown the Newtonian scheme to be of limited application. It is also relevant to show that a mechanical universe allowed the possibility of a narrow 'deist' view of a creator God.

AO2 This should give a brief religious evaluation of eighteenth-century deism, with comments about the way in which theism is broader in its view of the nature and action of God.

2. What significance, if any, would a well-established 'theory of everything' have for religious belief?

AO1 This requires a general appreciation of the way in which relativity leads to the idea that, in theory, it should be possible to find a single theory to account for the features of the universe.

AO2 You would then need to consider whether such an overall theory was the equivalent of Aquinas' uncaused cause and so on, and whether it would satisfy what people look for in the idea of 'God'.

Further questions

1 Do you think it is possible to be a 'religious nonbeliever', as Einstein claimed?

2 Would discovery of the Higgs Boson reveal a creator God?

THE ORIGINS OF THE UNIVERSE

Chapter checklist

The issue of how and when the world was created is central to the debate between scientists and those who take ancient religious writings literally. We shall therefore look both at scientific theories about the origins of the universe and at religious teachings, along with their responses to one another.

Key word

Cosmology: the study of the nature of the universe as a whole.

Theories about the nature and origins of the universe (whether they are ancient, medieval or modern) carry with them implications for understanding how humanity fits into their overall scheme of things, and whether it can have any lasting significance. Quite apart from any religious theories of creation, this fact alone places cosmology at the heart of issues connecting religion and science.

1 The dimensions of the universe

The twentieth century saw a dramatic change in the understanding of the dimensions and age of the universe. In this, as in many areas of science, details are always being revised, so the figures here should be taken only as a general guide.

The universe is estimated to consist of probably about 100 billion galaxies, each composed of stars and gas clouds. Our own galaxy (the central area of which is represented by the stars of the Milky Way) is spiral in shape and rotates. It is thought to contain between 200 and 400 billion stars and is about 100,000 light years in diameter and 10,000 light years thick. Our Sun is a smallish star, about 32,000 light years from the centre of the galaxy.

The next galaxy – Andromeda – is 2.44 million light years away and heading in our direction, so that, in all likelihood, the two galaxies will eventually merge. At the other extreme, the furthest galaxy to be observed has been called Abell, and appears to be 13.2 billion light

Key word

Light year: the distance travelled by light in a year, at a speed of 300,000 kilometres per second.

Key thought

In December 1997, astronomers witnessed the biggest explosion since the 'Big Bang' (see below), a blast of high-energy gamma radiation, lasting for one second and releasing as much energy as all the stars in the known universe put together. Yet it took place in a region only about 160 km across. The light from the explosion took about 12 billion years to reach Earth. In other words, it took place 8 billion years before the Earth was formed. The universe as a whole is a violent and inhospitable place. How do you find a religious concept of creation that copes with events and dimensions such as these?

years away. However, since it has been moving away from us since its light started to travel in our direction, it is now about 40 billion light years away from us.

But it is the content of the universe that is even more remarkable than its size. The matter we can detect – in other words, all these galaxies and their stars and dust clouds – comprises only about four per cent of the universe. The rest – seventy per cent dark energy and twenty-six per cent dark matter – cannot be detected directly but is thought to exist, for without it the structure of the universe would not make sense. And beyond and behind all that, there are the low-energy photons of the cosmic background radiation, at 3 degrees above absolute zero. These photons are about a billion times more numerous than the atoms that form the visible galaxies. Overall, the universe is a very strange and very empty place.

But equally strange is the way in which space and time are related. To look out into space is also to look back in time. If I observe a galaxy 10 million light years away, I observe it as it was 10 million years ago (when the light from it started its journey towards me), not as it is now. Imagine observers placed at different points in the universe, all looking at the Earth. They would see – unfolding in their present – events which are in our past. From nearby stars in our own galaxy, they see the building of medieval cathedrals or Egyptian pyramids. From stars at the far side of our galaxy, they see only primitive man. From the nearest galaxy cluster to ours (8 million light years away), it is too early for an observer to see even man-like apes, and from galaxies more than 5 billion light years away (less than half way across the known universe) there is nothing to be seen here but clouds of cosmic dust, for our Sun and its planets have not yet been formed.

And what of life itself, as we imagine observing it from these distances? It is but a chance and fleeting film of blue and green upon a tiny planet, lost in one of a billion galaxies. And all this matter is but an exception to the rule of emptiness, grains of sand spread thinly through a void.

Just as we now see Newton's laws as applying to a very limited set of conditions as found on Earth, so our theories about the visible universe are equally parochial, and will almost certainly need to be revised from time to time. The universe remains far less understood than we would like to admit.

a) World without end?

Following the Second Law of Thermodynamics, the universe should gradually dissipate its energy and end up in a state of total entropy (uniform disorder) and heat death. On the other hand, it is possible that, as the universe continues to expand, it will reach a point at which the energy of expansion is reduced to a point at which it is balanced by the gravitational pull, and at that point the universe would start to contract, eventually imploding. But whatever the fate of the universe, the Earth has a limited life, for as the Sun uses up its fuel it will change into a 'red giant', incinerating and absorbing the Earth as it does so. Even this is a distant prospect, for, at about 5 billion years of age, the Sun is only about half way through its present life.

But can scientific projections about the end of the Earth have any significance for religion? Christian imagery of the end of the world and of Christ returning to judge people operates on a totally different imaginative scale from scientific predictions about universal heat death. It originates from a time when the Earth was seen as the centre of the universe. The only really significant issue here is whether language about the end of the world needs to be taken literally, or whether it is a way of expressing those values that the religion holds to be 'final', in the sense of ultimate.

b) The limits of what can be known

It is important to recognise that the nature and dimensions of the universe are determined by the faculties by which we perceive it. There is a theoretical limit to what can be known. It is not merely that, one day, we will develop a telescope that will get us 'beyond' the known universe, it is that the universe and our way of experiencing it are bound up together.

Einstein suggested that the universe could be seen as a 'hypersphere'. If you start at a point on the surface of a sphere and move off in any direction, you never come to an edge, although the actual surface of the sphere is finite. In the same way, Einstein suggested that you could move through a finite universe without reaching an edge, eventually returning to your starting point. So, from the perspective of someone within a finite universe, it might appear infinite.

And this, of course, is a significant question for religious thinkers – for an infinite and eternal universe does not seem to allow any space or time for an external creator. We cannot get 'outside' the universe. The deist idea of an external creator and designer (see page 28) is simply illogical, in that an external 'God' would be entirely unknowable.

2 The Big Bang theory

Key word

Big Bang: a popular way of describing the event, about 13.7 billion years ago, that marks the origins of the present known universe.

Evidence for the past state of the universe is gained by observing trends in the present and projecting them backwards. At this moment, it can be observed that the galaxies are flying apart, and those furthest away from us are moving away faster than those nearer to us. From this we infer that at one time all the galaxies were closer together, and that they are moving apart in all directions.

On that basis, we can tell how far away a galaxy is by how fast it is moving away from us. The spectrum of light changes if the body being observed is moving away at very great speed. In 1929, E. P. Hubble observed a 'red shift' in the light coming from distant galaxies, which led to the theory that the universe is expanding in all directions. From the speed of expansion, it is possible to calculate the age of the universe.

It is therefore generally believed that the universe started with a 'hot Big Bang' about 13.7 billion years ago, the point from which the present universe expanded out in an explosion of enormous energy and heat from apparently zero size but infinite density. At this point – generally referred to as a 'space–time singularity' – all the general theories of physics break down.

In an ordinary explosion, matter is flung outwards *through* space. In the 'Big Bang', however, what we know as space and time are created simultaneously with that event. It is a point *from which* space and time have come, not a point *within* space and time. It is as though we are inside an expanding bubble.

What is clear is that our present universe was shaped by events that took place in the first few milliseconds of its existence, during which there was a sudden inflation and in which some of the basic features and constants were determined.

It can be argued that, in those first moments, there could have been other universes formed – as it was, it happened to form ours.

Stephen Hawking (whose *A Brief History of Time* remains a fascinating and readable introduction to this subject) argues that the space–time singularity is not the *start* of the universe. We cannot say that there was nothing before or outside the singularity, simply because words like 'before' and 'outside' have no meaning in that context.

This theory then predicts that at one time all the matter in the universe was spread out uniformly as a hot gas. This gradually cooled and condensed to form stars and galaxies. In the 1960s background microwave radiation at 3 degrees above absolute zero was found throughout the universe, and this is thought to be the remnant of the heat from that early phase. The theory also predicted the existence throughout the universe of stable, light elements (including, principally, hydrogen) produced at the earliest stage (unlike heavier elements, which were formed later in stars), and this has been found to be the case.

What the Big Bang theory did not explain is how the structures of the present universe came into being – for if the hot gas was absolutely smooth, it would have cooled in an absolutely uniform way. Clearly, there had to be a lumpiness in the initial hot plasma which allowed the formation of stars and galaxies as it cooled.

Key thought

None of this is intuitive, and it is proved only by the use of very elaborate mathematics, but it gives an idea of the sort of issues about the origin of the universe that occupy scientists today.

Key question

Posed by Stephen Hawking:
So long as the universe had a beginning, we could suppose it had a creator. But if the universe is really completely self-contained, having no boundary or edge, it would have neither beginning nor end: it would simply be. What place, then, for a creator?

A BRIEF HISTORY OF TIME

Key quotes

Professor Neil Turok who developed the idea of the 'instanton' commented:
Many people ask whether this has implications for the existence of a creator or divine intervention. Personally I don't think it does. But if a divine being wanted to create a universe, the simplest way to do it would be to use our instanton.
THE DAILY TELEGRAPH, 14 MARCH 1998

The big bang cries out for a divine explanation. It forces the conclusion that nature had a defined beginning. I cannot see how nature could have created itself. Only a supernatural force that is outside of space and time could have done that.

FRANCIS COUSINS,
THE LANGUAGE OF GOD

The next development came with particle physics and the quest to understand how it is that particles get their mass. Combining this with Einstein's equations describing the way the universe expanded led to a new theory for the very earliest moments – the 'inflation' stage – the point at which energy and matter seemed to appear from nothing. It was triggered by what is called an 'instanton' – a microscopic object of extreme density, but without any 'before' or 'outside', but capable of expanding into an infinite universe. This is why the detection of a sub-atomic particle (called the Higgs Boson), which is thought to hold the secret to the formation of mass, is so important for discovering why the universe started, and why so much money and effort is currently being put into discovering it (see page 57).

Modern cosmology is a fascinating and ever-developing branch of study. The Big Bang may have been triggered by what is called an 'instanton', a point of fleeting existence, outside time and space, which immediately triggers an infinite, expanding, open universe. For our purposes, however, such details do not matter. The fact is that science has established a generally accepted theory for the origin and structure of the universe, a theory which is compatible with the best available evidence.

How does this theory relate to religious ideas of a creator? The first thing is the obvious problem for any idea of divine creation of a universe that has no beginning or end, or, indeed, a universe that is infinite. It tends to deprive 'God' of a place to be, or – more significantly from a scientific point of view – it deprives 'God' of any possible evidence for or against his existence, for all evidence will be limited to the world.

An alternative view is that though these theories show *the way* the world was formed, they do not say *why* it was formed or *by whom*. It would therefore seem perfectly reasonable to suggest that belief in God can be held alongside this modern view of the origins of the universe. By not being able to speak of these things, this view leaves open the possibility of a divine creator.

But there are religious people who would take this one step further, namely that, even if the universe was created according to the standard 'Big Bang' theory, there needs to be some external, *supernatural* force in order to explain itself – and that, of course, takes it beyond the realm upon which science can comment. It also takes it into the realm that is beyond the limits of human reason and experience, and one that the atheist will say is irrelevant.

3 The anthropic principle

Key question

Does the structure of the universe make it inevitable that human life should appear and, if so, what conclusions might be drawn from this?

Key words

Fine tuning: the argument (often associated with the anthropic principle) that the original constants determining the development of the universe are exactly what is needed for the universe to exist.

Anthropic principle: the argument that the initial conditions and structure of the universe had to be exactly as they were in order for humankind to develop.

There are certain fundamental features of the universe that have enabled it to develop in the particular way it has. But if the universe had developed differently, we wouldn't have the galaxies we have, nor suns and planets and an Earth capable of sustaining life. In other words, if things were different, we would not be here: that much is clear. But what conclusions should we draw from that fact? One answer to this question is known as 'the anthropic principle'.

Imagine a universe in which one or another of the fundamental constants of physics is altered by a few percent one way or the other. Man could never come into being in such a universe. That is the central point of the anthropic principle. According to this principle, a life-giving factor lies at the centre of the whole machinery and design of the world.

(J. D. Barrow and F. J. Tipler,
The Anthropic Cosmological Principle, 1986)

There are weak and strong versions of the anthropic principle:

- **Weak:** If the major constants of the universe were different, we would not be here, life would not have evolved.
- **Strong:** The universe contains within itself the potential for life, such that it was impossible for human life not to have appeared.

The weak version causes no problems; it merely states the obvious. But the strong form seems to imply that the whole development of the universe took place in the way that it did *so that* human life should appear.

Stephen Hawking's comments:

[The strong anthropic principle] … runs against the tide of the whole history of science. We have developed from the geocentric cosmologies of Ptolemy and his forebears, through the heliocentric cosmology of Copernicus and Galileo, to the modern picture in which the earth is a medium-sized planet orbiting around an average star in the outer suburbs of an ordinary spiral galaxy, which is itself only one of about a million million galaxies in the observable universe. Yet the strong anthropic principle would claim that this whole vast construction exists simply for our sake. This is very hard to believe. Our Solar System is certainly a prerequisite for our existence, and one might extend this to the whole of our galaxy to allow for an earlier generation of stars that created the heavier elements. But there does not seem to be any need for all those other galaxies, nor for the universe to be so uniform and similar in every direction on the large scale.

(*A Brief History of Time*)

Key quote

The existence of a universe as we know it rests upon a knife edge of improbability.

FRANCIS COLLINS, *THE LANGUAGE OF GOD*, 2007

Key thought

Consider the two statements:

'Fancy seeing you here this early, you *must* have got the 6.30 train!'

'You *must* get the 6.30 train!'

Whilst the second is a command, the first is merely a deduction. The strong version of the anthropic principle starts with a deduction, and then makes it appear to be a command.

Key word

Providence: the view that God has created the universe in such a way as to provide what is needed for life, and especially for human life.

The logic behind the anthropic principle would seem to run like this:

- If the universe were different, we would not be here.
- Everything in the universe is determined causally, once the initial parameters are set.
- Therefore, given the parameters, life had to evolve.

Nothing wrong with that, but the implication is then made that the initial parameters *had* to be what they are. Here we come against the problem of chance and necessity. Consider the chance of two people meeting in the street:

- Everything I have ever been, and everything that has happened in the world, has contributed in some way to the fact that I am in this place at this time.
- The same thing applies to you.
- Therefore the odds *against* us meeting up by chance are almost infinite, since they depend upon an almost infinite number of prior events.

But, given that every event has a cause, then, given the way the world is, it is *inevitable* that we should meet. *Thus, in a world in which everything interconnects, every event is both highly unlikely but (with hindsight) also inevitable.*

Extreme care therefore needs to be taken by anyone who thinks that the anthropic principle can be taken as evidence for a designer God, or as in some way placing humankind in a privileged position within the universe, and therefore as a sign of God's providence. The logic of the weak form of the argument does not warrant either conclusion, and although the strong version could support them, its logic is flawed.

Science itself has moved rather beyond the parameters set by a straightforward anthropic argument. It was claimed that, if any of the fundamental constants were different, then the world would not have been able to form as it did, and we would not be here. However, some (e.g. Victor Stenger in *God: The Failed Hypothesis*) have pointed out that most who claim this work on the basis of trying to change *one* of the constants while leaving the others as they are. That, of course, fails to produce a viable universe. However, it can be argued that, if *all* the constants are allowed to vary alongside one another, there are a number of different values that can equally produce a viable universe. So it is far from certain that we need to have a fixed set of values in order to have a universe. Of course, we needed to have exactly those values in order to have exactly *this* universe – but that is really a trivial point; it simply says that the universe is as it is because it is as it is!

Key thought

THE END OF IT ALL ...

Earth is regularly hit by objects from space. Mostly they are small and a majority burn up as they enter Earth's atmosphere. About once every 100 years something of 50 metres in size causes devastation over a significant area – as happened in 1908 in Tunguska, Siberia. There are, however, about 1500 asteroids of more than a kilometre in diameter that cross Earth's orbit. When one of those hits Earth, the destruction is global. It is believed that a asteroid of about that size, impacting the Earth on the Yucatan peninsular in central America, wiped out the dinosaurs about 65 million years ago – although that interpretation of the general extinction at that time is challenged, particularly since there have been other global extinctions in the past, the biggest of which (about 250 million years ago) is thought to have wiped out ninety-five per cent of living species.

It would be illogical to believe that no asteroid of that size will ever hit the Earth in the future. If it does, there is a good chance that humankind, along with other species, will be either largely or completely destroyed.

How does that possibility square with those interpretations of the anthropic principle (or with religious views about the purpose and place of humankind within creation) that suggest that humankind has a privileged place in the scheme of things?

4 Creationist views

In the early part of the twentieth century, a movement arose among conservative Protestant Christians in the United States that sought to defend the fundamentals of the Christian religion, as it saw them, against the threats of liberal theology. This became known as fundamentalism, and over time it focused its attention on defending certain key doctrines, notably the literal truth of the account of creation given in the Book of Genesis.

Fundamentalists were also opposed to the idea of evolution. From the time when Darwin published *The Origin of Species*, and even earlier in the debates about geology, there had been some opposition to all such theories from those who were committed to a literal understanding of creation as described in Genesis. Some emphasised the need for divine agency, others the distinctiveness and special creation of species and particularly of humankind. In Chapter 7 we shall look at the particular question of evolution, but, for now, we need to be aware of general fundamentalist opposition to scientific accounts of the origins of the universe, a view known as creationism.

Creationists are those who hold a literal (or near literal) interpretation of scripture. They may accept that one thing was created before another, but will usually argue that this is implied by

Key thought

In discussing the origins of the universe, or evolution, it is important to recognise that the creationist, literal interpretation of Genesis is a recent and minority phenomenon, although one that is growing. Most religious thinkers – including St Augustine in the fourth century (see pages 12–13) – were far more sophisticated in their appreciation of the Bible and its language. Sadly, those who come to the religion and science debate via the atheist criticism of religion might get the impression that all genuinely religious people were creationist fundamentalists, and to dismiss the more intellectually based and balanced views of religion.

Key word

Creation science: the term used for the range of arguments put forward from about the 1970s to argue for an understanding of nature based on the idea of creation by God, including the idea of intelligent design. Although backed by religious fundamentalism, it claims to be science rather than religion. See also Chapter 7, section 6, for the creationist challenge to evolution by natural selection.

Key thought

The key feature of the debate between those who accept the scientific basis of evolution and the creationist is that of the source of authority. For scientists, authority comes from the impartial analysis of experimental data and the acceptability of a theory by the scientific community. For creationists, ultimate authority comes from the Bible.

the six 'days' of creation in Genesis – each day being taken to refer to a long period of time, rather than a literal 24 hours. What creationists want to preserve is the uniqueness of the creation of humankind, and the direct action of God to bring it about.

Those who keep to a literal understanding of Genesis are sometimes referred to as 'Young Earth creationists', since they believe that the Earth is only a few thousand years old. In spite of all the evidence to the contrary, this view is held by a substantial number of people, particularly in the United States, where is it taught within some evangelical churches. It is the view that suggests that humans lived alongside dinosaurs, denies that the fossil record shows any intermediate stages between one species and another, and may even claim that the fossils were deposited as a result of the biblical flood. This form of creationism, although widely held, is broadly incompatible with mainstream science, where the evidence for the age of the Earth and the slow process of evolution is overwhelming.

Conservative creationists, holding to a strictly literal interpretation of Genesis, claim that the world was created exactly as described in the Bible. Scientific theories about the age of rocks, for example, are seen as quite irrelevant, on the grounds that God might have planted such evidence for things appearing to have existed long before their actual creation, perhaps in order to test people's faith. This sort of argument dates back to the nineteenth century, in the early debates about evolution, and includes such questions as whether the trees in the Garden of Eden could have had 'tree rings' (i.e. the appearance of having grown for a number of years in order to reach their mature size), or whether Adam had a navel, and – if so – for what purpose.

Progressive creationists suggest that the world was made as described in Genesis, but that the reference to 'day' in the account does not literally mean 24 hours, but a more general description of each successive period of time. This may allow someone to accept scientific data about the age of the Earth without thereby being disloyal to the Genesis account.

An additional problem for a creationist, if the world was really created only a few thousand years ago, is to account for all the evidence to the contrary, from galaxies that are millions of light years away from us, to the apparent age of rock strata and fossils. One possibility is that God planted all such evidence as a test of faith. However, as has been pointed out (e.g. by Francis Collins in *The Language of God*), this would make God the Great Deceiver! Is it really likely that God, if he exists, would be concerned to organise such a massive act of subterfuge, deliberately going against all knowledge acquired by reason and evidence?

Key thought

The idea of a deceiving God is exactly the sort of folly of which Augustine warned in his *On the Literal Meaning of Genesis*. Not only does it portray God as deceiving and manipulative, which is against what most Christians would see as a moral approach to life, but, by focusing on something so clearly nonsensical, it may discourage a serious consideration of other ways of interpreting scriptures and religious teachings.

Sometimes alternative explanations are offered for the scientific findings. Thus, for example, the Australian creationist Barry Setterfield has argued that the speed of light has diminished since creation, which accounts for the 'red shift' phenomenon (which was used to predict the speed at which galaxies were moving apart, and thereby the age of the universe), and that the universe is therefore much younger than was thought.

But even when creationists present alternative hypotheses which appear to be scientific, or which are based on scientific evidence, it is clear that they are not seeking an answer with an open mind – their aim is to prove the case for what they hold to be true on religious grounds.

The issue of how to interpret Genesis was seen as fraught with difficulties long before the Big Bang theory. Saint Augustine wrote *On the Literal Meaning of Genesis*, having felt that his earlier analogical view of the account of creation was inadequate. But he certainly did not take the account 'literally' in the sense that some modern creationists do. He acknowledged the difficulty with understanding the true meaning of some of the words used, and argued that some of the words had been used in an obscure way in order to stimulate our thought. Thus he holds that terms such as 'light' and 'day' have a spiritual rather than a physical meaning. Overall, he cautions against taking too rigid a view, but suggests that each person should take whatever interpretation he or she can grasp.

Augustine was particularly concerned that those outside the Christian faith, hearing someone expound Genesis in a way that is clearly against reason and evidence, will cause the faith to be ridiculed. In effect, he is worried that people will dismiss the serious teaching of Genesis because it is presented in a way that is open to criticism.

5 Creatio ex nihilo

Key word

Gnostic: used of those who claimed secret 'knowledge' as the basis for their religious views. A common feature of the gnostic point of view was that the world itself was an evil place, out of which the spiritual elite would be saved. The orthodox counter to this was to proclaim the absolute creative freedom of God, and therefore the inherent goodness of his creation.

In the scriptures, God is described as the creator of the heavens and the Earth. Sometimes this is done quite graphically, as when he is said to make Adam out of the dust of the Earth and then breathe life into him, or when making Eve out of one of Adam's ribs. Other accounts (and we need to remember that there are at least two accounts of creation in the Jewish scriptures) have God simply speaking a word for things to come into being.

The key feature of these biblical accounts is to establish the absolute power and authority of God – setting him against the gods of other people, who are seen as limited in power. It also fixes the relationship between human beings and the created order. Humankind is given authority over the other creatures, and is allowed to exploit the Earth, which is there for the benefit of humans.

Key thought

In quantum theory, sub-atomic particles come into existence without having a particular antecedent cause, and a quantum understanding of gravity might therefore conceive of space–time being created out of nothing with the same unpredictability. Quantum theory therefore appears to be more compatible with the idea of *creatio ex nihilo* than the older Newtonian physics. These ideas are discussed by Paul Davies in his book *God and the New Physics*. However, care needs to be taken with all such arguments – for they compare a scientific observation with a religious doctrine which originated at a very different time, and for a particular purpose, namely to proclaim the goodness of creation and the absolute power of God.

Central to the Christian doctrine of creation is that God created the world out of nothing (*creatio ex nihilo*) rather than out of any pre-existing material. This was important in the fourth century, to distinguish orthodox Christianity from the 'gnostic' view that matter was evil – since it could not have been evil if directly created by God.

To appreciate its later significance, consider the *deist* view of God as an external agent and designer. For the deist, God and the world are two separate things, in that God is located 'outside' the world. In a sense, his being there or not makes no difference to the workings of the world – it is like a machine that he has created and left to run on its own. The *theist* view, by contrast, is of a God who is both immanent within and yet transcends the world. Whatever is happening in the world is therefore seen as part of God's activity – there is no separate material order with which he is not concerned.

The crucial thing to appreciate is that the Christian doctrine of creation is about *agency* (that God made the world) whereas the 'Big Bang' and other theories are about the *mechanisms* by which the world came into existence. A theist could quite well say that the 'Big Bang' was the mechanism by which the world came about, whilst still holding that God was the agent of that creation.

6 God: 'being itself' or external agent?

Key thought

What kind of 'God' is compatible with the dimensions and nature of the universe?

In *God: The Failed Hypothesis* (2007) Victor Stenger argued that God should be detectable by scientific means, so that, if there is no convincing evidence for God's existence, then the claim that he exists should be seen as a failed hypothesis in scientific terms.

Notice his presuppositions here. He assumes that God is the sort of entity that exists alongside others in the world, and for the existence of which it is valid to set up tests and examine the resulting evidence. Many religious believers would say that is an inadequate way of thinking about God – God is not one thing alongside others.

On the other hand, Stenger has a valid point when he argues that, if religious people are going to make claims about God (that his activity is to be seen in the design of things, or in action to produce miracles, for example), then those claims are about matters that science can investigate, to see if there are explanations of them that do not involve the idea of God – and hence that claims for God's activity are open to be challenged if there is no evidence for them.

The alternative approach is to say that God is not within the physical world as an object for which there could be evidence. But in that case, the only logical thing is to see 'God' as a word that describes a fundamental aspect of reality, or reality looked at in a personal way, or even a shorthand way of expressing a sense of purpose and meaning.

Cross-reference

This issue will emerge again in Chapter 7, as we examine the ideas of evolution and design. Complexity becomes 'design' when you have a designer, which implies an agent of design (i.e. God) separate from the complex object that appears to have been designed.

Key words

Existentialism: a philosophy relating to the sense of meaning and purpose in human life.
Pantheism: the view that the world itself is to be worshipped as God.
Panentheism: the view that all things exist within God and he within them.
Theism: the view of God held by Judaism, Christianity and Islam. God is said to be both within the world and yet transcends it.
Immanence: used of God as found within the world.
Transcendence: used of God as found beyond the world of sense experience.

What seems inconsistent, and therefore open to Stenger's criticism, is to try to make God both *immune from* the normal process of scientific investigation, and at the same time make claims for his activity that clearly imply a physical difference in the world – and hence something that science *should* be able to investigate.

By contrast, John Macquarrie (in his *Principles of Christian Theology*) takes an existential approach to the doctrine of creation, by examining what it says about human meaning and values. He argues that, if you believe yourself to be a creature made by God, you will be answerable to him, subject to his demands and feel yourself to be a recipient of his grace. The opposite view (which would be taken by someone who did not see God as the agent of creation) would be one in which you feel yourself to be independent, self-directing, and not answerable to anything outside yourself.

Clearly, by turning the issue of creation into an existential one, he separates its religious importance from any scientific view about the origins of the universe. The existential approach makes factual claims about God and creation irrelevant – all that matters is *the personal significance of that belief.*

As we have already seen, **deism** is the view that God is an external creator and designer, no longer found within the world, but thought to be its original designer and cause. The actual mechanism by which the world unfolds is irrelevant to such a belief; all that is required is the sense that the world displays some form of intelligent design.

Equally, a pantheist has few problems with views about the origin of the world, since this belief simply identifies God and the world – theories about the world are theories about God, simply that.

For the theist and panentheist, however, the matter is not quite that simple. Both views present God as immanent within and yet transcending the physical world (and **panentheism** is really only an extension of **theism**, emphasising the **immanence** of God). The problem here is that religions generally describe God as engaged and active within the world, taking a continuing creative role. How does that role (or that agency) square with scientific explanations? One of the problems here concerns the temptation to 'locate' God's activity in gaps in the scientific explanation of things.

God of the gaps

As science explains something, there seems no need to suggest that it was brought about by God. The more science explains, the smaller become the gaps into which God's activity can be fitted. The classic example of this was the reply given by the mathematician Pierre Laplace (1749–1827) who, when asked where God came into his calculations of the planetary orbits, declared 'I have no need of that hypothesis'.

Thus, for example, Aquinas needed an 'unmoved mover' to explain present movement. With Newton, however, all movement follows fixed laws, and objects continue either at rest or in uniform motion in a straight line unless acted upon by external forces. Present movement is therefore entirely predictable. At most, all that is required is some initial force to start the whole thing going. God is therefore located right outside such a mechanical universe.

As the explanation of cosmic origins improves, or medical knowledge explains an unexpected recovery from disease, so the 'gaps' into which God can be fitted diminish. The problem was put very succinctly by John Habgood:

> *In a world made up of objects, God has to be thought of either as an object or as a concept. If the former, there seems to be less and less space for him in our scheme of things as scientific knowledge advances; if the latter, religion is a private fantasy.*

(*Religion and Science*, 1964)

Key people

Paul Tillich (1886–1965)
From being a Protestant military chaplain to the German forces in the First World War, Tillich went on to become a secular philosopher, and then, escaping Nazi Germany, he settled in the United States. He worked to reinterpret the Christian faith in terms that reflected issues of personal meaning and commitment, using language and ideas that had been developed by existentialist philosophers, concerning the personal nature of 'being'.

Key thought

The question then is not whether there is 'something' called God that might or might not exist, but rather whether the word 'God' is a helpful one in describing reality.

Key question

Being itself – reality itself – is a term for that which exists. If that is what you call 'God', then fine. But does that actually square with what most religious people believe? Do they think of God as reality itself, or do they actually think of him as in some way separate from the physical world and able to intervene within it?

The theologian Paul Tillich argued that God should be described as 'being itself' rather than 'a being', and this is relevant to the 'gaps' dilemma. If God is thought of as a being among others, there becomes less and less room for him. But the very idea of God being an object within the world could, from a theistic point of view, be regarded as *idolatry*. The whole essence of classical theism is that God is both immanent (within the world) and transcendent (beyond the world). Such a balance does not allow God to be identified with any one thing. Hence, the quest for a 'gap' for God is fundamentally mistaken. *Any god found in a gap could not be the 'God' of classical theism!* In describing God as 'being itself', Tillich and others were avoiding any attempt to consider God as one entity alongside others – and therefore as something about which it would make sense to argue that he did or did not exist. If 'God' is 'being itself', rather than 'a being' among others, it implies that the word 'God' is being used to describe reality itself – the same reality that is described by science and experienced personally.

Clearly, science, as a method of investigating the world, does not require the use of the word 'God' in its explanations; individual scientists may do, and – naturally enough – individual believers may find it a key word for their experience of encountering and relating to the world, and understanding their place within it.

Summary diagram

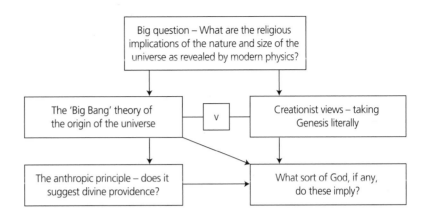

Study guide

By the end of this chapter you should appreciate something of the dimensions of the universe and the Big Bang theory, as presented by modern science, and have considered the religious responses to this – both in terms of the way in which ancient scriptures should be interpreted, and also in terms of whether the idea of 'God' is compatible with such a universe, and – if so – what it says about his nature.

Revision checklist ✓

Can you explain ...?

■ Why observations of the universe suggest that it originated in a 'Big Bang'.
■ What is meant by a 'creationist' view of the origin of the universe, and on what grounds it challenges the scientific view.
■ Why Tillich called God 'being itself' rather than 'a being'.

Do you know ...?

■ What is meant by the 'anthropic principle'.
■ What *creatio ex nihilo* means, and why theism does not accept the idea of pre-existing matter, separate from its creator.

Give arguments for and against ...

■ The view that a modern, scientific understanding of the universe is incompatible with belief in God.

Examples of essay questions

1. Explain what is meant by 'the God of the gaps', and how this problem has come about. Suggest how a religious person might present a concept of God that did not require a 'gap'.

AO1 A straightforward exposition of the way in which this approach has come about should be accompanied by some examples of 'gaps' into which the action of God has been fitted.

AO2 This requires an appreciation of the limited nature of a 'gap' approach to God, and an outline of ideas such as 'immanence' or '*creatio ex nihilo*' which suggest God's presence and action are seen everywhere, rather than in gaps.

2. How far has modern science shown that the universe does not need a creator?

AO1 A response to this question should show an awareness of versions of the 'Big Bang' theory and the natural explanations it provides for the existence and nature of the universe.

AO2 This requires a discussion of the role of God as creator, and whether that is seen as external to the developing universe (as in deism) or integral within it (as in theism). In the latter case, the further question is whether that immanent action of a creator is compatible with a natural theory of origins.

Further questions

1 What are the religious implications of the view of the universe revealed by modern cosmology?

2 The anthropic principle is problematic for supporting religious claims of divine providence. Discuss.

3 The 'God-of-the-gaps problem' helps shift religious focus from an external 'deist' view of God to one that involves both transcendence and immanence. Discuss.

7 EVOLUTION AND DESIGN

Chapter checklist ✓

Logically following on from questions of the origin of the universe come those concerning purpose and design. Here there is a clear clash between those who see God's agency in the appearance of design in the world, and those who see complex organisms and systems as the product of natural processes.

The theory of evolution, based on natural selection, provides a natural mechanism to explain the appearance of 'design' as an on-going feature of nature. Hence it throws the debate between science and those who hold a literal view of the Bible, with each species created separately by God, into sharpest relief.

1 Purpose, direction and providence

In looking at the history of the development of science and also the methods used by science and religion, it is clear that science is based on a study of evidence, and the framing of hypotheses concerning the fundamental structures and principles upon which the universe, as we experience it, is formed.

It cannot get *beyond* the sphere of the evidence upon which it is based. By contrast, we have seen that religion often makes claims that are not based on empirical evidence. In speaking about God, or an afterlife, it goes beyond the realm of science. Of course, this leaves open the question of whether anything can be known outside experience – in other words, whether there is any valid 'supernatural' knowledge, and how such knowledge might be validated.

As long as science keeps to the analysis of empirical evidence, and religion keeps to personal stories and inspirational concepts which are seen as totally 'beyond' the realm of science, then there are few clashes between them. The real problems occur, however, when religion makes claims that appear to depend upon evidence that can also be examined by science.

Problems occur, therefore, as soon as religion claims that the universe displays purpose and direction, or that the way in which it has developed is such as to provide special care for humankind. Such claims might be open to being checked by empirical evidence: does humankind, for example, have a special, guaranteed or permanent place in the universal scheme of things? But they are religious claims, rather than scientific ones, for *purpose implies the intention of an intelligent being*, and – for a theist – such purpose is the intention of God.

A key religious term for the discussion of purpose and direction is 'providence'. This is the belief that God has in some way chosen to create, nurture and sustain humankind: that life is not possible merely by some chance, or by the impersonal process of evolution, but is something guided by God for his own purpose in dealing with humankind. Some religious thinkers make this a key factor in their understanding of God. In his book *Science and Providence* (1989), John Polkinghorne comments:

> *Though the evolutionary history of life has proved marvellously fertile, it shows scant concern for individual species, let along particular creatures … Without special providence, the idea of a personal God is emptied of content. Whatever it may mean to use personal language of God in an analogical sense, it surely cannot mean less than we experience of our own personhood, which is not content with general benevolence but seeks to meet individual needs in individual ways.*

The religious difficulty with the idea of special providence is that it attempts to ascribe divine purpose to some events but not to others. Thus, if an aircraft crashes, killing all but one of its occupants, the lone survivor might ascribe his or her survival to divine providence. But that same act of special providence (given the idea of an omnipotent God) implies responsibility for the death of all the others. *Those who feel themselves specially singled out can do so only at the expense of others who are not so favoured.*

Every claim for special providence implies a selective field of vision or interest. Thus, from the point of view of mammals in general, and human beings in particular, the destruction of the dinosaurs might seem to have been providential. But if that is the case, then surely another species, now awaiting its chance to flourish, may herald the destruction of the human species in exactly the same way.

The implication of this for the whole issue of God and evolution is therefore clear. Evolution provides the structure, the machinery, by which species develop. It is a process by which random changes afford an opportunity for some individuals in a species to develop more than

Key word

Providence: the view that God has created the universe in such a way as to provide what is needed for life, and especially for human life.

Key question

Is belief in divine providence reasonable in the light of evolution, and of all the sufferings of contingent existence?

Key thoughts

In other words, it is not enough to accept a general providence – that God in some way established the evolutionary process in order to create humankind – but also that a personal creator would want to react to particular situations.

Winning a lottery is providential only in the eyes of the person who wins; others see it rather differently!

others, to reproduce more successfully, and thus to influence future generations and the gradual shift in the character of the species.

In the eyes of a secular scientist like Richard Dawkins, that process is magnificent and utterly awe inspiring. The most complex and wonderful creatures emerge from a long process that involves the application of just a few basic principles. That spectacle of self-generated life does not require an external creator. Equally, it makes little sense, given the huge 'wastage' of life that is involved in every evolutionary advance, to ascribe its direction to the special intervention of God.

However, Polkinghorne concludes:

Key question

At what point (The Black Death? The trenches of the First World War? The Holocaust? The tsunami that struck south-east Asia? 9/11? A single child dying of cancer?) would it have been 'fussy' for God to have intervened?

> *The Christian understanding of providence steers a course between a facile optimism and a fatalistic pessimism. God does not fussily intervene to deliver us from all discomfort but neither is he the impotent beholder of cosmic history. Patiently, subtly, with infinite respect for the creation with which he has to deal, he is at work within the flexibility of its process.*
>
> (*Science and Providence*)

Of course, a major question here is exactly how you tell the difference between a patient and subtle providence and no providence at all!

2 Geology

One of the key features of the way in which the world was perceived in medieval times was the balance between that which changed and that which was permanent. Individual creatures were born and died, all particular things known to the senses were subject to change and decay, but (following the influence of Plato) the essence of each species was fixed, and these essences (the Platonic 'forms') defined each individual thing's place and purpose within the universe.

What is more, there was a long tradition – including Augustine, Aquinas, Newton and Paley – of thinkers who saw the wonders of the world as leading the mind naturally to the idea of an intelligent designer and creator: God. God's purpose was revealed in the essence of each species, and just as the flight of the arrow (to use Aquinas' example) made no sense without an archer to shoot it, so the wonderful way in which living things were put together made no sense without a divine designer.

Indeed, until the end of the eighteenth century, it was commonly believed that the world was less than 6000 years old, that each species had been created separately, and that no species could develop out of another. Such beliefs, which were in line with a literal interpretation of scriptures, were to be challenged by developments within geology and biology during the nineteenth century. The world was no longer seen as fixed, pre-designed and handed down by a divine creator, but as a process of evolution which over long periods of time appeared to be designing itself.

Smith and Lyell

William Smith (1769–1839), a drainage engineer and amateur geologist, collected information about rock strata and the fossils contained in them. He observed that the deeper strata were older than those nearer the surface, and that the fossils in the strata showed life forms very different from anything found in his own day. He concluded from this that there must have been many successive acts of creation. Geology had become a science capable of revealing history, for Smith's analysis showed successive stages of life on Earth.

Responding to the biblical account of creation, Smith took the six days referred to in Genesis as six geological periods, rather than literal 24-hour days. He therefore accepted separate acts of creation, but saw them as taking place successively. This view gave rise to a number of 'catastrophe' theories, in which there were a succession of acts of creation, followed by catastrophes, the latest of which had been the flood as described in Genesis.

In his book *Principles of Geology* (published between 1830 and 1833), Charles Lyell (1797–1875) took a very different view. He argued that the process of geological change was going on all the time, and therefore that there was no need to posit separate acts of creation in order to account for the different strata and fossils. This interpretation of change as a continuous process was termed 'uniformitarianism'.

Whether by a series of creations and catastrophes, or a uniform process of change, the new perspective given by nineteenth-century geology did not in itself cause theological problems. It simply required a reinterpretation of the mechanics of creation, and it still allowed for the agency of God in designing and creating species.

It is important to recognise that this successive creation of life forms is not the same thing as evolution. These geological developments were more easily accommodated within traditional beliefs. In *Foot-prints of the Creator*, a book that was very popular when published in 1847, Hugh Miller, a Scottish geologist, argued that the biblical pattern of creation followed by a fall could be seen throughout the geological record. His point was that species did not improve with the passing of time; rather, as in the Bible, they were created perfect and subsequently 'fell'. It made no sense to argue that humankind developed from earlier life forms, for that would have implied progress, rather than creation and fall.

Miller's book was published three years after another, more controversial one. Chambers' *The Vestiges of the Natural History of Creation* (1844) had been published anonymously, and spoke of the

Key thought

With hindsight, it is interesting that Smith's idea of successive catastrophes and creations, dismissed once a theory of continuous evolution emerged, might come closer to the truth than was once thought. We now know that there have been major global extinctions of species – the latest of which, about 65 million years ago, wiped out the dinosaurs – after which the planet's fauna gradually recovered.

Key thought

The significant point made by Miller was that the idea of humankind developing from other species would, he felt, prevent people from thinking of themselves as spiritual creatures with immortal souls. He therefore separated off his geology from the more controversial ideas about evolution.

development and introduction of new species throughout geological time, challenging both the ideas of biblical creation and also the uniqueness of humankind. But at this stage, Chambers did not have a mechanism with which to explain how such change could come about.

An attempt to reconcile the discoveries of geologists with the account of creation given in Genesis was made by Philip Gosse in *Omphalos* (1857). He asks whether God could have been trying to deceive by creating rocks in the Garden of Eden which contained fossils, or fully grown trees with tree rings, as though they had been growing for years. He concluded that the trees in Eden would have to have had rings, for that is simply what fully grown trees are like. Similarly, Adam would have had a navel – although, clearly, he would not have needed to have one, being created directly by God.

We see in this book, and in other arguments of this time, a struggle to recognise the growing evidence of a long history of creation, with the basic features of the biblical creation.

> **Key thought**
>
> Some challenged Genesis more directly. A few years earlier (in 1852) Herbert Spencer had argued that if there were indeed no less than 10 million different species that existed or had existed on Earth, which was the more likely: that there had been 10 million individual acts of creation, or that by continual modification and changed circumstances, 10 million different varieties had been produced and were still being produced?

3 Darwin and natural selection

> **Key question**
>
> The theory of natural selection provides a natural and straightforward mechanism that explains the appearance of 'design'. This renders the idea of a 'designer' *unnecessary*. But does that automatically imply that the idea was *wrong*?

> **Key people**
>
> **Charles Darwin (1809–82)**
> The son of a doctor and grandson of Erasmus Darwin (an early evolutionary thinker), Darwin studied medicine at Edinburgh and then went to Cambridge, intending to be ordained. In 1831 he was offered a place on board *HMS Beagle* as a naturalist, in order to explore wildlife in South America. He returned in 1836, convinced, by the peculiarity of the variety of species he had seen, that one species must indeed develop out of another. He spent the next twenty years gathering evidence and developing his theory of natural selection, publishing *The Origin of Species* in 1859.

In spite of the controversy that had been taking place over the previous decades concerning Genesis and the geological record, Charles Darwin's *The Origin of Species* (1859) was hugely controversial because for the first time it suggested a mechanism – natural selection – by which species might develop.

The existing theory about changes in species, propounded by Lamark earlier in the century, was that they changed very gradually as a result of the influence of environment and diet. In order for this theory to work, it was essential that characteristics acquired during a lifetime could be passed on to the next generation (generally known as the 'theory of acquired characteristics'). Charles Darwin first used but later rejected this theory.

The key to Darwin's work was the theory of 'natural selection'. This, with hindsight, seems remarkably simple, but it was a radical step. It is simply this:

- Within any species there are individual members whose particular characteristics help them to survive better than others.
- Those who survive to adulthood are able to breed, passing on those characteristics to the next generation.
- By this mechanism, with successive generations, those characteristics which improve the chance of survival will be found in an increasing number of individuals within the species, for they will be the ones who survive to breed.

Key people

Erasmus Darwin (1731–1802)
Darwin held that all life formed a single living filament and that new species could develop out of older ones, and that humans were the culmination of the evolutionary progress to date, but that they could continue to develop. In many respects, he held views that were to be controversial when his grandson, Charles, discovered natural selection as the mechanism for such change. His main publication is *Zoonomia* (1794), a book on medicine, with his evolutionary views attached.

Jean Baptiste de Lamark (1744–1829)
Lamark categorised species according to their physical complexity and believed that evolution was moving in the direction of increased complexity. The fundamental difference between Lamark and Charles Darwin was that Lamark held that physical characteristics acquired during one's lifetime could be passed on to one's descendants – a commonly held view at the time.

Thomas Malthus (1766–1834)
Malthus observed that populations were controlled by the amount of food available, and where there was competition for available food, only the strongest were able to survive. He thus provided a key component in the theory of natural selection.

● Hence the characteristics of a species are gradually modified in favour of those that facilitate survival. Thus nature selects those fittest to survive.

He illustrated this theory by pointing out that people had long bred domestic animals for particular characteristics.

In this, he was using a theory about populations and survival produced by Thomas Malthus in *Essays on the Principle of Population* (1798). Here Malthus had argued that animals and plants produce more offspring than can possibly survive, and that their numbers are controlled by lack of food and/or space. Thus the environment is the limiting factor on the numbers of survivors within any one species. This – given the apparently chance variations in characteristics within a species – provided the mechanism Darwin needed.

This mechanism (backed up now by our understanding of genetics, and therefore the process by which small errors in the copying of genes lead to the chance variations) is very simple. In fact Professor Steve Jones, writing about his book *Almost Like a Whale* (1999), describes life as 'a series of successful mistakes'. That is exactly what evolution is, and it highlights why, as a theory, it is so amazing but also so threatening to those who see God as the designer of everything.

Notice how problematic such a theory could be for religious people. First of all it challenged the unique status of the human species, but even more crucially, it challenged the notion of purpose in creation. Species flourish or decline depending upon their ability to adapt to their environments. There is no externally determined *purpose* in their survival. In other words, the whole of the natural world is based on a process of change that is fundamentally impersonal. That appeared to be contrary to the idea of a God who created the world for a purpose, and whose will is being worked out within it.

a) Was Darwin religious?

When it came to interpreting the Bible, Darwin found that he could not take it literally. In particular he felt that, if God were to act upon the world, he would do it through the operation of natural laws, rather than intervene by way of miracles. He concluded that those of earlier times were more credulous than those of his own day.

In this, he was no different from many people in the eighteenth and nineteenth centuries, when – as we saw above – the emphasis was on a rational approach to religion. The fundamental difference between Darwin's position and that of the deists of a century earlier was that he could not have accepted the 'argument from design', since his theory of natural selection took away the need for an external designer.

Key quote

Darwin himself admitted that looking at an organ as complex and sensitive as the eye, it seemed almost absurd to think that it could have been produced through natural selection. But if …

the eye does vary ever so slightly, and the variations be inherited, which is certainly the case; and if any variation or modification in the organ be ever useful to an animal under changing conditions of life, then the difficulty of believing that a perfect and complex eye could be formed by natural selection, though insuperable to our imagination, can hardly be considered real.

ON THE ORIGIN OF SPECIES

Key quote

There is grandeur in this view of life, with its several powers having been originally breathed by the Creator into a few forms or into one; and that while this planet has gone cycling on according to the forced law of gravity, from so simple a beginning endless forms most beautiful have been and are being evolved.

THE ORIGIN OF SPECIES,
CONCLUDING REMARK

Darwin retained belief in God, and expressed a sense of wonder that many would see as a form of natural religion. This passage comes from the end of *The Origin of Species*:

> *It is interesting to contemplate an entangled bank, clothed with many plants of many kinds, with birds singing on the bushes, with various insects flitting about, and with worms crawling through the damp earth, and to reflect that these elaborately constructed forms, so different from each other, and dependent on each other in so complex a manner, have all been produced by laws acting around us. These laws, taken in the largest sense, being Growth with Reproduction; Inheritance which is almost implied by Reproduction; Variability from the indirect and direct action of the external conditions of life, and from use and disuse; a Ratio of Increase so high as to lead to a Struggle for Life, and as a consequence to Natural Selection, entailing Divergence of Character and the Extinction of less-improved forms. Thus, from the war of nature, from famine and death, the most exalted object which we are capable of conceiving, namely the production of the higher animals, directly follows.*

Although in many ways this simply sums up the process by which his theory of natural selection operates, it also gives a general sense of wonder at the natural order itself. The question remains whether such a religious sense of wonder – which was later to be expressed by Einstein – constitutes religion, or whether the term 'religion' should be reserved for those systems which require belief in supernatural agencies.

But whatever one's conclusions about the nature of Darwin's religious beliefs, there can be no doubt that, in spite of all the controversies caused by his theory, he was greatly respected, and formed a focus for much of the scientific and intellectual endeavour of his day. He died in 1882 and was buried in Westminster Abbey.

b) Reactions to Darwin

Darwin's theory was supported by Alfred Wallace (who had come independently to similar conclusions about evolution), by the geologist Sir Charles Lyell (see above), by the humanist T. H. Huxley and others. It was opposed by those who, for religious or other reasons, thought it important to defend the idea of fixed, independently created species.

It is quite wrong to assume that all scientists were for Darwin and religious people against. Amongst the churchmen who supported him was Charles Kingsley, whose comment – that he considered it as noble a conception of God that he created creatures capable of self-development as to think of God needing to intervene in order to produce new species – was quoted by Darwin

Key thoughts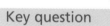

It was, in any case, a time of controversy within the Church of England. *Essays and Reviews*, a collection of seven articles by seven different authors calling for a more liberal approach to religious belief, was published in 1860. Among other things the debate it stirred up concerned the flexibility with which the Bible should be interpreted – a crucial issue in looking at Genesis in the light of geology and the theory of natural selection.

We should keep in mind that the initial reaction of religious people to Darwin's discovery was favourable, most being content to see it, rather as Darwin himself claimed, as simply an alternative way in which the creator had chosen to create.

Key question

Is religion committed to a dualistic view of reality, with a separate, sacred world? The impact of Darwin's theory was to promote a naturalistic view – that there is one world, not two. As Don Cupitt comments:

After Darwin we are bound in the end to be committed to a nondualistic view of both the human being and the world.

AFTER GOD, 1997

in the preface to his second edition. He also had the support of R. W. Church, Aubrey Moore and F. D. Maurice, all influential in the Church at that time.

There was, of course, much criticism as well. In a review of *The Origin of Species* in *Quarterly Review* (July 1860), Bishop Wilberforce argued that there was no immediate evidence to show that, even in domesticated animals, there was a change in their species. Mockingly, the review asks: 'Is it credible that all favourable varieties of turnips are tending to become men …?' At the British Association meeting in Oxford in 1860 there was a debate on this between Wilberforce and T. H. Huxley. Famously, Wilberforce asked Huxley whether it was through his grandfather or grandmother that he claimed his descent from an ape.

Not all criticism focused on the religious problems of setting Darwin's theory alongside the creation account in Genesis. There was also criticism that there appeared to be no direct evidence for transitional states between species within the fossil record itself.

Since Darwin's time there have been two general answers to this from within the scientific community. One is that the fossil record is very limited in scope, and the chances of finding a fossil of an intermediate state would be relatively rare – although in recent times more fossil evidence for this is emerging. The other argument is that the process of evolution may not be uniform, but consists in a short burst of change, followed by long periods of stability. This would explain the rarity of intermediate states, simply on a statistical basis.

c) Implications for 'God'

How may religious people relate the theory of evolution by natural selection to the idea of God? There are a number of possibilities here:

- A theistic 'interventionist' approach suggests that, although evolution can account for the development of species, there are moments when God intervenes directly. Thus, for example, the official Catholic teaching (in *Humani Generis*, 1950) stated that the body of Adam may have been developed by a process of natural selection from other species, but that his soul was created directly by God. One of the problems here is that it sees God as occupying a 'gap' in scientific explanation, and – as we have seen – this creates further problems as science gradually extends human knowledge.
- A different approach, but also one taken from a Catholic standpoint, comes from Karl Rahner (in *Hominisation*, 1965), who argues that human beings are made wholly by evolution, but also – from a religious point of view – wholly by God. In such an approach, God and evolution are not seen as mutually exclusive explanations of human origins, but evolution is seen as a mechanism through which God operates.

- The philosopher Henri Bergson (1859–1941) argued, in his book *Creative Evolution*, that there was a 'life force' guiding the evolutionary process, and that this propelled all species forward in a great movement towards the future. This view is generally termed 'vitalism', and at one time it was thought to provide a way of seeing the action of God within the evolutionary process. However, developments in twentieth-century biology, showing the basis for evolution to be by random genetic mutation, make the idea of a 'life force' redundant.

- It is also possible to see evolution itself as having a definite purpose and direction through the interpretation given of it by religion. In this way science and religion complement one another in their assessment of the evolutionary process. Examples of this are found in A. R. Peacocke, *Science and the Christian Experiment* (1971), and L. C. Birch, *Nature and God* (1965), who sees God's activity as determining the 'final causes' of everything (to use terminology originally coined by Aristotle; see above, page 10).

All of these approaches raise a fundamental dilemma, which appears time and again in religion and science debates. How is it possible to relate an autonomous universe with what religious people want to claim as the action of God?

4 DNA

Key thought

The human body may be made up of water and other chemicals, but these *do not define what it is to be human*, nor can the laws under which their molecules operate give much of a guide to how the whole human being operates.

Discoveries in the 1950s led to a study of biology at the molecular level, where it seemed to follow the laws of physics. It was popularly believed that biology could simply be reduced to physics – in other words, that the bodies of living things could be understood by reducing them to their individual molecules, each obeying physical laws.

Against this it has been argued (e.g. by A. R. Peacocke and P. Davies) that physics and chemistry cannot give a full account of living things. Biological life is far more complex than the molecules of which it is comprised; therefore different concepts are needed for each level of complexity. Living things can no more be described in terms of individual cells than a painting can be appreciated by analysing threads of canvas or brushstrokes of paint.

The discovery of *deoxyribonucleic acid* (*DNA*) in 1953 provided the basis for modern molecular biology. All living things are formed out of chemical substances (waters, sugars, fats, etc.). Of these, the nucleic acids (RNA and DNA) and proteins control the way in which living cells are put together. *Proteins* are made up of *amino acids*, whose production depends on information provided by DNA. In the nucleus

Key thoughts

Only about two per cent of the nucleotide string is used to code the genes that produce our proteins. The function of the apparently surplus DNA is an issue that has not yet been resolved.

One practical use of such information is in forensic identification. Since the genetic code is unique to each person, but contained in every cell of his or her body, it is possible to identify someone from a small sample of cells from any part of their body (e.g. small quantities of blood from the scene of a crime). The genetic analysis of a sample from a crime scene can be compared with that of a suspect.

Each person is born with about 100 mutations. Most of these will have no direct effect on the protein-producing genes, but with each generation they will accumulate. The total bank of human DNA, contained in every cell of every human being, is thus constantly changing, and we – as a result – are evolving.

From a scientific point of view, creationism is simply wrong, for it makes a distinction between humans and other species which is simply not in line with the common body of genetic information through which all species are formed. Species are not as different from one another as creationists wish to assert.

of each cell (except for sperm, egg and red blood cells) are 23 pairs of *chromosomes*, which contain the DNA, made up of two strands of chemical units called *nucleotides*, spiralled into a double helix. Information contained in the sequence of nucleotides (sections of which are called *genes*) determines how the protein is made. Human DNA has about 3.4 billion nucleotides, and about 25,000 genes.

Thus, every cell (of which the human body has about 30 trillion) contains the information needed to reproduce every other cell in the body.

The term 'genetic' is used for the information contained in the DNA, which determines the character of every organism. A *mutation* takes place when one of the amino acids in a protein chain is changed for another. If a mutation takes place in a germ cell (a cell that will go on to form a sperm or egg), which is rare, it can be passed on to children; mostly they occur in non-germ cells, and lead to an irregular growth in cell tissue. 'Mistakes' are rare, because the chromosomes work in pairs, and a good copy from one chromosome usually dominates a defective copy from the other.

Darwin's theory of natural selection showed how, given a number of variations within individuals in a species, those with particular advantages would survive, breed and influence the process of change in that species. What Darwin did not know was the reason for the random occurrence of varieties, some useful, some not. We now know that the reason for variety is that the genetic code is not always copied exactly, leading to the occasional mutations, some of which survive and reproduce because they work well alongside the rest of the genes in the 'gene pool' of that particular species.

There is also a fundamental similarity at the molecular level between all forms of life. The building blocks of the genetic code are universal, and the genetic differences between species are often quite small. At one time, the evidence for evolution depended on the fossil record; nowadays it comes also from genetics. Certain genes play very similar roles in different species, and this suggests that, if you trace those species back, you will come to a common ancestor, from which each has inherited its particular genetic material. Along with the mechanism of natural selection, it shows just how interconnected and similar all life is.

The genetic basis of evolution is sometimes presented as though the whole process were random, thus denying any sense of direction. This is not correct. The gene mutations that arise do so at random, but once those mutations have appeared, some succeed and some do not. *In other words, there is a self-selection process that operates, depending on the ability of that particular mutation to survive in its environment.* Change thus builds on those mutations that have given a positive advantage.

It is important to get an imaginative grasp on the immensity of new information revealed by genetics. Consider human development from conception to birth. Gradually, from a fertilised egg and then a tiny cluster of cells, the material differentiates, the organs form, and a human being slowly takes shape. That development is an amazing process, ascribable, from a religious point of view, to a divine designer and creator. Yet we know that the fertilised egg actually contains all the genetic information to produce that unique human being. What is more, the information that programmes that development shows parallels with the information that will go to produce countless other species. Life is a matter of 3.4 billion bits of information, stored on the DNA's double helix; the purpose of most of it is yet unknown, but within it are the genes which contain all the instructions for building a human being.

5 Social Darwinism

Key people

Herbert Spencer (1820–1903)
Spencer applied the theory of evolution to social development, coining the term 'the survival of the fittest' in his *Principles of Biology* (1864). He saw society as an organism that would develop and become more complex as time went on, and believed that a view of the perfecting of humankind, and the explanation of everything in terms of scientific laws, would replace conventional religious beliefs.

Herbert Spencer is often regarded as a social Darwinist, although in fact his view of evolution was rather different from Darwin's, since he thought society was developing towards some perfect final state.

Cross-reference

For more on the 'naturalistic fallacy' see *Ethical Theory*, Chapter 3, and *An Introduction to Philosophy and Ethics*, Chapter 8, section 4.

Darwin himself had examined the implications of his theory for human development. In *The Descent of Man* (1871) and *The Expression of the Emotions* (1872), he suggested that human mental ability and social behaviour could be shown to have the same sort of historical development as the human body. This is termed 'social Darwinism'.

The development of social Darwinism is particularly associated with the work of Herbert Spencer, who went beyond anything Darwin himself had suggested, and was therefore opposed by T. H. Huxley, one of Darwin's staunchest supporters.

The implication of natural selection, according to Spencer, was that human society should follow the struggle for survival in nature. Thus those not strong enough to live should be allowed to die. He opposed the Poor Laws and state education, since these benefited those least able to take care of themselves. His evolutionary ethic was based on the proposition that whatever makes the totality of life greater must be good; whatever diminishes life must be bad.

In opposing Spencer, T. H. Huxley (and others) put forward the general point that facts about evolution pointed to what *did in fact happen*, but that did not imply that they could be used as a basis for saying what *ought to happen*. This is a crucial point for ethics, where it is generally argued (e.g. by Hume, but later, at the beginning of the twentieth century, by G. E. Moore) that in general you cannot derive an 'ought' from an 'is' – in what is known as the 'naturalistic fallacy'.

Key quote

Evolution is to the social sciences as statues are to birds; a convenient platform upon which to deposit badly-digested ideas. Biology tells us that we evolved, but when it comes to what makes us human is largely beside the point. There might be inborn drives for rape or for greed, but Homo sapiens, uniquely, need not defer to them. This has not stopped those who try to explain society from debasing Darwinism to support their creed.

PROFESSOR STEVE JONES, *DAILY TELEGRAPH*, 16 AUGUST 1999

In considering Darwin, it is crucially important not to confuse his arguments, or the theory of natural selection, with Spencer's 'survival of the fittest' morality. To do so would be to give the theory implications which Darwin himself did not intend. Whether such morality is implied by Darwin's theory is, of course, a separate matter, but it should not be seen as the only possible interpretation of his work.

Richard Dawkins' book *The Selfish Gene* illustrates a further implication of the genetic basis of evolution. According to Dawkins, our genes are inherently 'selfish', not in some morally pejorative sense, but simply because their task is to promote survival and successful reproduction. The human bodies through which they operate can therefore be thought of as their 'survival suits'.

What you cannot do (and Dawkins has made this quite clear) is somehow take the imagery too literally (individual genes cannot be, in a literal sense, 'selfish' – for that applies at a very different level of human behaviour), nor should one move from biological theory to social theorising (e.g. as Spencer did on the basis of Darwin). Thus Dawkins is *not* saying that genetic theory justifies 'selfish' behaviour on the human level: a misunderstanding arising out of the title of his book.

6 The design argument

Cross-references

Philosophy of Religion, Chapter 5, and *Introduction to Philosophy and Ethics*, Chapter 4, section a.

Many Christians have argued that the predictable and ordered world shown by Newton illustrated that the world was the handiwork of an intelligent designer. In an example used by William Paley in *Natural Theology*, published in 1802, if one came across a watch lying on the ground, one would conclude, having examined the intricacy of its mechanism, that it was the product of an intelligent designer. If any part of the mechanism were ordered differently, the whole thing would fail to work. And it did not matter that one might not understand absolutely everything about the mechanism, or that it sometimes failed to operate as expected – the key thing was that, unlike a stone, a watch mechanism is clearly organised in order to achieve a particular goal, the telling of time. By analogy, this argument suggested that a study of the complex and purposeful features of nature would lead to the conclusion that it, too, was the product of an intelligent designer: God.

But somewhat earlier, the philosopher David Hume, who considered that all knowledge was derived from experience, had already criticised this popular notion of design. He argued that, in a situation where there are a vast number of possibilities, only those that actually work will survive. Therefore what appears now as the product of an external intelligent designer may in fact be the one

Key thoughts

The design argument enabled eighteenth-century rationalists to accept a place for religion. The implication of Hume's criticism was that design did not require a religious explanation, and therefore (like Laplace and his calculation of the planetary orbits) he no longer needed to use God to explain what was observed.

The idea of the universe as a watch (made famous by William Paley) originally came from Isaac Newton. He argued that the mechanism of the world was like that of a watch, where everything linked to everything else. Hence the first movement – or prime cause of movement – must come from outside the watch. This is God as the *deus 'ex machina'* – literally 'outside the machine'.

To the argument that you can't have a design without a designer, the answer is that you can have complexity without necessarily calling it a 'design'.

surviving example of a large number of variations – surviving because it was the one that worked and stabilised. Evidence could point to a working complexity, but could not take a step beyond that to show an external designer.

This simple but devastating argument sets the tone for later debates, most notably over Darwin's theory of natural selection. Hume's argument (that, given a very large number of possibilities, that which works will survive) is effectively given a specific mechanism in natural selection. In its twentieth-century version, given random genetic damage, only those new genes that are successfully reproduced can survive and flourish.

The problem here, for the religion and science debate, is that religious believers were led to defend an inadequate idea of God (deism) based on an outdated philosophy (Aristotle's concept of final cause and design) in order to support their beliefs. They believed that if the idea of the world as a purposively designed mechanism, pointing to a divine craftsman, were overturned, there would be no further scope for God or religion.

It is therefore important to distinguish between two questions:

- Is the world 'designed' by some external agency or is it self-designing?
- Does religious belief depend upon the answer to that first question?

The assumption that was made during many of the eighteenth- and nineteenth-century debates on this was that the answer to this second question is that religion does indeed depend upon the world being 'designed'.

The 'design argument' claims that the appearance of design implies a designer. However, there is a fundamental flaw in the logic here – and one that was shown by David Hume's criticism. 'Design' is not the same thing as, say, 'complexity' or 'beauty'. To say that something shows signs of design already implies that there is a designer.

The key question is therefore whether the complex and wonderful way in which creatures function within their environment, and have bodies that work to maintain them in existence, are actually signs of 'design' or simply signs that – over many generations of trial and error – they have developed progressively more complex ways of self-organising.

A key religious question in assessing evolution from a Christian point of view (and we need to be clear that this is a matter of Christian doctrinal authority, not a feature of religion in general) is the nature and authority of scripture, and particularly Genesis.

Those who hold that the truth of scripture can only be affirmed if it is interpreted literally hold that creation must take place over a period of one week in what was (from the geological perspective) the very recent past. Those maintaining this position need to explain the appearance of more ancient life forms, for example within the fossil records. Hence the attempts by Gosse, for example, to stand where Adam stood and see newly made trees complete with rings that gave the impression of age.

Those who do not require, as an act of faith, that all scripture should be taken literally are likely to interpret the scriptural image as a poetic or symbolic way of expressing reality. Hence the argument that the days of creation in Genesis are not to be thought of as periods of 24 hours, but as eras. This follows the tradition of Galileo, Bacon and others, who in the days of the rise of science had seen truth as being contained in two separate books – the Book of Scripture and the Book of Nature – which were essentially complementary, rather than opposed. Such a view allows the possibility of affirming the essential meaning of Genesis, while also accepting the long time scale required for the process of evolution.

It is crucial here to see exactly what happens to God in these situations: deism was subsequently regarded by many Christians as an inadequate view of God, because it made him external to the universe, rather than bound up with what happened within it. God was an agent of events only in a very detached and secondary way.

The same issue arises in considering evolution. Should God be considered to be simply the originator of the system that then operates by evolution, or should he be regarded as operating directly through the agency of evolution?

If so, one needs to examine why a God who is regarded as good and loving should use a mechanism which allows progress only *at the cost of an almost infinite amount of suffering* – for it is only the non-survival to adulthood of a majority that allows a minority to breed and influence the future of the species.

Key thought

EYES

For most creatures, being able to see is key to finding food and avoiding predators. Eyes give an evolutionary advantage. It is curious to reflect then that there appear to be eight different mechanisms by which 'eyes' work, and eyes have developed independently many times. There are thus many different designs of eye.

- Does that argue against an intelligent designer, on the grounds that eyes have come about on a trial and error basis?
- Or does it suggest that each different form of eye is separately designed to meet the needs of each particular species?

Key people

Richard Swinburne (b. 1934)

Nolloth Professor of the Philosophy of the Christian Religion until his retirement in 2002, Swinburne continues to write and lecture on the philosophy of religion, recently publishing second editions of his *Faith and Reason* and *The Existence of God*.

Key thought

This can then be linked to the religious implications of the anthropic principle (see pages 69–70) – if the world is 'fine tuned', the most economical explanation for that phenomenon is the existence of an intelligent and purposeful creator who is doing the tuning.

Key quote

So I suggest that the order of the world is evidence of the existence of God both because its occurrence would be very improbable a priori and also because, in virtue of his postulated character, he has very good, apparently overriding, reason for making an orderly universe, if he makes a universe at all.

R. SWINBURNE,
THE EXISTENCE OF GOD, 2004

Swinburne's way of presenting the design argument is based on the fact that science finds regularities in the universe, which it codifies in terms of 'laws of nature'. He argues that, although the nature of the universe may be explained in terms of these laws of nature, the laws themselves are not explicable by science. In other words, we know there is regularity, but we do not know *why* there is regularity.

Explanations can be either scientific or personal – so if there is no scientific explanation of *why* there are such laws or regularities, the only possible explanation must be in terms of the purposes of an intelligent being. Hence he argues that the simplest (and therefore the preferred) explanation is that the universe is designed by a purposeful creator.

But there are problems with this approach. First of all, we have to consider whether general patterns (of the sort that lead us to formulate laws of nature) are really only explained with reference to an *external* intelligence. One might argue that, in a world that is changing and evolving as a result of a limited number of fundamental forces, regularity is more to be expected than randomness.

But secondly, does an explanation need an explanation? The laws of nature do not *explain* regularity, they simply *describe* it. It is an open question whether any *explanation* is needed. Once you accept that it is, then you are already set up to argue in favour of an external intelligence to explain it – for the world does not contain within itself an explanation of itself. Why can we not say that the world is as it is, and leave it at that?

To the challenge that nature itself can produce the complexity seen in living things, Swinburne's answer is that as humans we have the ability to make machines which make other things. Hence the fact that nature may account for the production of design does not in itself render invalid the idea that God might have made nature to make these 'designed' things. *The problem with that, of course, is that there can be a regress in the argument – we can go back one stage and ask who designed God, and so on.*

To the claim that orderliness in the world is inherently improbable, one might ask:

- How, unless you have observed a number of different worlds, at least some of which show no signs of order, can you claim that order is improbable?

To the claim that the postulated character of God makes him likely to create an orderly rather than a disorganised universe, one might ask:

- Unless you have a source of information about the nature of God that is quite *separate from* any sense of him as an orderly creator (which is based on the experience of order in the world), how – without arguing in a circle – can you then claim that his character is such as to suggest that he will create an orderly world?

Key thought

There have been some
fundamental disagreements –
between Stephen Jay Gould and
Richard Dawkins, for example – on
whether natural selection works
only on the level of genes (so says
Dawkins) or also at the level of
organisms and even species. Notice
that, as in all good science, there
can be genuine disagreements
about how to interpret data, and
strongly held views between
competing approaches.

One of the most persuasive opponents of the design argument is Richard Dawkins. In his best-selling book *The Blind Watchmaker*, he examines the way in which more and more complex organisms can be formed by the application of one or two quite simple principles. The force of his argument is that you do not have to have some *external* source of rationality or design in order to explain evolution. This he further developed in *Climbing Mount Improbable*, where what looks an impossible feat of design becomes quite inevitable, given sufficient time and sufficient numbers.

Thus the natural feature of life to self-organise and the inevitability of the rise of more and more complex forms over a period of time are linked directly with the genetic basis of life. Our uniqueness and our 'design' are given through the very complex genetic code that determines how every cell in our body is to develop.

7 Intelligent design

Key thoughts

In Chapter 6 we looked at the
general issue of creationism, which
represented a response by
fundamentalist churches to the
scientific view of the origins of the
world. The contrast between the
unique status of humankind as
understood by a literal reading of
Genesis, and the view of it given by
evolution, was a key feature of the
creationist argument.

The main problems with the theory
of natural selection from a
fundamentalist point of view were:

● The concept of 'God' as a
creator and designer was
made redundant.
● The universe appeared to have
no purpose, and the direction
of evolution was determined
by an impersonal mechanism
of survival and breeding.

In the nineteenth century, the religious reception given to Darwin's ideas was mixed – some Church leaders welcoming his ideas, others opposing them. Central to much of that opposition was the linking of humankind to other species, and the sense that humans were no longer unique and special in the order of things.

It was really only in the 1920s, particularly in the southern states in the USA, that a major clash occurred between the idea of evolution and a literalist approach to the biblical account of creation. In particular it took the form of a challenge to the idea of evolution being taught in schools – a debate that continues to the present day.

The fundamentalist response to evolution was generally based on a literal interpretation of scripture. At the 1925 'Monkey Trial' in Tennessee, John Scopes was prosecuted and fined for teaching evolution, when state law required only the biblical account of creation to be taught in schools (his conviction was later overturned by the State Supreme Court). Even in the 1980s, fundamentalists in Louisiana campaigned for the biblical account of creation to be given equal emphasis in schools alongside the theory of evolution, and a note in textbooks points out that evolution should be considered a theory rather than a fact. The Catholic Church is more liberal in its approach, since in 1996 the Pope said that evolution could be recognised as 'more than a hypothesis'. Yet in the United States opposition to evolution continues, and in August 1999 the Kansas State Board of Education voted to remove it from the school curriculum. It is estimated that up to 100 million Americans believe that God created humankind very much as it appears today, and did so within the last 10,000 years.

Key word

Irreducible complexity: the argument that the complexity of organisms cannot be fully explained by reducing them to their constituent parts. Because specific parts have specific functions, it is difficult to see how they could have evolved, since their final form is required for the whole complex body to work. To use a popular example, a mousetrap will only work when the final pin is put in place. How then can a mousetrap evolve? A 'nearly mousetrap' would not work at all!

The issue of intelligent design in the broad sense refers to the idea that individual species are the product of an intelligent designer. This, in turn, is seen as the alternative to Darwin's view that natural selection provided the mechanism by which species could evolve and which therefore explained the apparent elements of design.

However, in recent years, intelligent design has come to refer to a rather more specific approach, initiated in 1991 by Philip Johnson's book *Darwin on Trial*, and associated particularly with the idea of *irreducible complexity*, an idea examined particularly by Michael Behe in his book *Darwin's Black Box* (1996).

The modern intelligent design position is essentially an attempt to defend religious faith against the challenge of secular science, which can be seen as encouraging materialist and atheist views. It focuses on the amazing complexity of living things, which display all the hallmarks of having been designed for a purpose. It suggests that natural selection cannot account for the way in which parts of organisms each have a very specific role to play within the complex whole.

One inherent problem with the irreducible complexity idea is that, as science progresses, it is more and more able to explain ways in which complex forms of life have come about. So, for example, biologists have shown that particular parts of the body change their function as the whole body evolves – so they do not have to be fully designed and developed for the body to work.

Hence 'irreducible complexity' and 'intelligent design' arguments fall into the 'God-of-the-gaps problem', where the need for divine intervention gradually retreats as knowledge increases.

8 Interpreting the evidence

We have looked at a number of ways in which God and evolutionary science can be related:

- *Either* the world is materially determined and wonderfully self-creating, and there is no God (except in the religious imagination, as a way of interpreting the world);
- *or* science is wrong when its conclusions differ from the teaching of the Bible, and evolution is either a mistaken theory, or has limited scope;
- *or* evolution explains the mechanism by which the world has developed, and God can be understood as being involved within, or as underlying, that process.

Key thought

Much has happened in biology since the original debates over natural selection, and genetics has shown that species are closely related, sharing genes that perform similar functions in very different bodies. It is amazing that many people today can, in the name of religion, reject such a vast amount of factual evidence. It illustrates the great power that religion can have to overcome reason and common sense, and also the general lack of appreciation of how science works and the methods it uses. But this may be partly because ordinary experience shows permanence rather than change – species *look* different; we do not *see* them evolving. The same could be said about the dimensions of the universe – for, looking up on a cloudless night, the stars appear as much fixed in their places today as they did for the medieval star-gazer.

Key thought

In criticising Richard Dawkins' *The God Delusion*, Alister McGrath (in *The Dawkins Delusion*, 2007) makes the important point that evidence needs to be examined objectively, recognising that there may be more than one valid interpretation and conclusion to be drawn from it. It is all too easy for those who have a particular belief, whether it be science's monopoly on truth, or the inerrancy of the biblical account of creation, to refuse to take seriously any alternative interpretation.

In evaluating these options, you may wish to consider the following questions:

1   What does religion mean by the 'supernatural'? Does the supernatural have to be totally *outside* the realm of natural causes? Is the supernatural necessary for religion?
2   God is spoken of as being both transcendent and immanent. How might the idea of immanence be used to show God *within* the evolutionary process?
3   In a sacrament, God is described as being present and active in an event which has a physical basis. Is it possible therefore to describe the relationship between God and the whole evolving world as 'sacramental'?

S. L. Jaki, in *Cosmos and Creator* (1980), argued that there is no way in which we can decide, from evidence alone, between blind mechanism and purposeful mechanism; purpose can only be seen once there is a prior belief in God as the rational creator. The world, as revealed by science, is contingent (i.e. it need not have existed at all), and in itself it appears to be meaningless. The world can only be thought of as a 'home', a rationally ordered cosmos, if a person first accepts the idea that it has a creator. This is linked to the main theme of Jaki's work, which is that science makes no sense without the belief that the world is a rationally ordered place, capable of being understood. He sees this as the common basis for both natural theology and science.

Here there is a particular example of the old question about the extent to which our ideas shape the world we experience. Until the nineteenth century, it was generally accepted that the scientific method was as 'objective' as possible, and that evidence should not be distorted because of the particular views of the scientist. That view has been modified during the last century only to the extent that it is recognised that the way in which we observe data influences that which we observe. And that caveat applies generally to the extremes of our experience – notably the area of sub-atomic particles. It cannot be taken as a general retreat from the attempt to assess evidence in an impartial way.

But it is important to take into account the function of religion in giving a sense of meaning and purpose. Its statements are *interpretations* of the world as much as claims about particular things *in* the world – and *interpreting the significance and value of something is a personal activity that need not conflict with the sort of evidence relevant to science*.

Key thought

Falling in love with someone can be exhaustively described in terms of psychological and biological urges, the operation of hormones and genetic predispositions and perhaps even social pressures. Yet such a description cannot do justice to the actual experience. It is not that there is 'something else' that is love. Love is simply the personal way of describing what happens. This distinction is common enough (described in terms of analysis or synthesis, of taking a reductionist or holistic view) but it remains central to these issues. To present God's creativity as somehow an *alternative* to evolution is doing the equivalent of making love an alternative to hormones.

The three questions given above raise fundamental issues about the nature of religious claims. Key to these is the question about what is meant by 'supernatural'. If it denotes causes and explanations which are conceived of as being of the same kind as those found within the universe, but somehow external to it, then the general view of science will always be that there can be no evidence for such things, and that the scientific view of the world sees no need to take them into account.

On the other hand, if 'supernatural' is taken in some way to mean an interpretation of, or way of encountering, the world, then there seems to be no reason why it should not exist alongside scientific explanations, since the two modes of thought and explanation are quite different.

Summary diagram

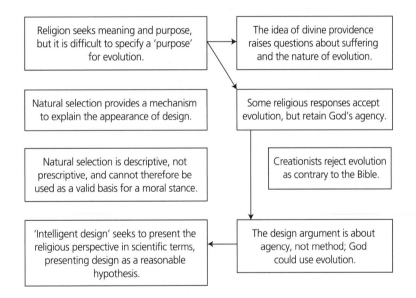

Study guide

By the end of this chapter you should understand the main features of evolution by means of natural selection, and have assessed the validity of religious arguments in favour of the idea that the world is designed by God, and that 'intelligent design' is a valid alternative to evolution.

Revision checklist ✓

Can you explain …?

- What is meant by natural selection and how it works.
- Why fundamentalists oppose the idea of evolution.

Do you know …?

- Why the discovery of DNA has strengthened the theory of evolution.
- What is meant by divine providence.

Give arguments for and against …

- The view that evolution by natural selection is compatible with belief in the existence of God.

Examples of essay questions

1. To what extent, and in what respects, can it be argued that humankind is unique? Illustrate your answer with reference to Darwin's theory of the origin of species.

AO1 The linking of species through the process of natural selection (and additionally through shared DNA) represents one side of this. The claims of religion that God created each species separately represents the other.

AO2 There are two evaluations to be made – first the *extent* of humankind's uniqueness (i.e. whether being *similar to* other species detracts from it, and whether having evolved from earlier forms also does so), and second the *respects* in which humankind may be seen as unique – language, the use of technology, brain power, etc.

2. 'There is grandeur in this view of life …' Do you agree with Darwin that his view of evolution, as set out in The Origin of Species, can express the grandeur of a process originated by God?

AO1 This requires an awareness of the scale of evolution as presented by Darwin, and the fact that he describes it as a process carried out by a divine creator. Can evolution be inspiring *in itself*?

AO2 The assessment needs to be made as to whether Darwin's theory actually detracts from the idea of a creator and designer God, or whether it is compatible with the idea of God using evolution as his design tool.

Further questions

1 Is evolution compatible with the idea of divine providence?

2 Discuss the implication for religious belief of Darwin's theory of natural selection. To what extent is it possible to argue that Darwin was genuinely religious?

FREEDOM AND DETERMINISM

Chapter checklist ✓

We examine the idea that science implies a determinist view of reality (namely that everything is, in theory, predictable) and consider whether this is correct and the issues such a view throws up for religion and morality.

Key word

Determinism: the philosophical view that all things are totally conditioned by antecedent causes, and that future events are therefore theoretically predictable.

The religious view of a world created and controlled by God, where things happen according to his will, and where human beings are free to act but responsible to God for what they do, appears to be incompatible with a scientific claim that all events are theoretically predictable, and thus not free to be other than they are.

1 A historical perspective

The first thinker to have tackled the issue of determinism was Democritus, a Greek philosopher of the fifth century BCE. He was one of the atomists (see also pages 8–9) who developed the idea – remarkable for that time, although commonplace to us – that everything consisted of atoms in space. He argued that objects existed independently of our observation of them, and that it was possible, in theory, to predict how each and every thing would behave.

He also came to the conclusion that atoms could not have emerged out of nothing, and that they were therefore eternal. However, individual atoms grouped together to form complex entities (all the objects of our visible world) which were constantly changing as their component atoms dispersed to form other things. In other words, you have an eternal, material world, in which all the things that we experience are composite and temporary collections of atoms.

This view of the universe (which was taken up by the Epicureans) created a problem for those who wanted to claim that people were

Key thought

The Epicureans took a rational and realistic view of human life. Since we are temporary, composite creatures, we might as well make the most of such happiness as can be had in this life, knowing that it will inevitably come to an end. In an impersonal universe, the prudent pursuit of pleasure would seem to be the best option.

Key question

Why should I be damned by God for something that God has already determined will happen?

Key quote

An intelligence knowing at any instant of time, all forces acting in nature, as well as the momentary positions of all things of which the universe consists, would be able to comprehend the motion of the largest bodies of the world and those of the smallest atoms in one simple formula, provided it were sufficiently powerful to subject all data to analysis; to it nothing would be uncertain, both future and past would be present before its eyes.

PIERRE LAPLACE (1749–1827),
QUOTED IN PAUL DAVIES,
SUPERFORCE, 1984

Am I free to choose my direction in life? Or am I more like a person on an escalator, gradually being carried along with everyone else in a pre-determined direction?

Key word

Cartesian dualism: Descartes' distinction between mind (unextended in space and known immediately) and matter (extended in space and known through experience).

free to act as they chose and that life had purpose and direction, for it saw the whole universe as a single determined mechanism, operating on impersonal laws.

The problem of freedom and determinism was given religious impetus by St Augustine, in connection with the nature of evil. He presented what was to become the traditional dilemma that, if God is omnipotent (all powerful) and omniscient (all knowing), he both knows and is able to control all that we do. How then can we be held responsible for any evil we do?

Augustine saw evil as a sign of the fallen nature of humankind, but because God gives people free will, they are responsible for whatever they do. On the other hand, in order to maintain the omniscience of God, he argued for predestination: that God knows already who is to be saved and who damned, and that we can do nothing to alter that judgement. Clearly, such views do not square easily with the notions of freedom, morality, conscience or justice.

With the rise of science, the mechanistic view of the universe given by Newtonian physics suggested that everything in the world may be described in terms of laws that operate with mathematical precision. If all the laws of nature were known, it would be possible to predict exactly what would happen in each and every situation in the future, given a complete knowledge of the world as it is now. Everything is determined.

Following the same scientific principles, any event that is unexpected is not generally ascribed to divine intervention, but is thought to have been caused by the operation of factors and laws that are not yet understood. Thus science assumes that everything has a cause – or indeed a large number of causes working together – which determine exactly what it is and how it has come about.

This view has implications both for human freedom and morality, and also for the idea of divine providence – God intervening in the world, setting aside its laws, for some special purpose.

The religious emphasis on the issue of freedom and determinism therefore moved on to take this mechanistic view into account. As a result of his systematic questioning of what we can know for certain, Descartes made a radical distinction between the physical and the mental worlds. I am a thinking being linked to a physical body that is part of a predictable, physical universe. His concern was to see how a mental operation (having a particular thought or desire, deciding to do something) could have a physical result.

Cartesian dualism and the rise of modern science resulted in the perception of a mechanical universe, totally conditioned and determined, every movement theoretically predictable, within which human beings had thoughts and desires, chose what to do and acted

Key question

If the physical universe is controlled by the laws of nature, how does my deciding to move my arm actually make that happen?

in a way that they experienced as being free. What is more, in order to be religious or moral, it seems absolutely necessary to be free to choose how to act. The fear, from a religious point of view, was that a totally conditioned universe would leave no place for either religion or morality.

2 Leibniz: God's chosen world

Key people

Gottfried Leibniz (1646–1715)
As a mathematician, Leibniz discovered calculus and invented a calculating machine. As a philosopher, he analysed the nature of substance, arguing that everything is divisible into its smallest possible parts (which he called 'monads') that had no extension and were therefore to be considered mental rather than physical. He saw God as a necessary being, ensuring that the otherwise separate monads work together to produce the world that we experience.

Leibniz considered that God was an eternal and infinite mind, who saw and determined everything in the created order and who had chosen to make the world exactly as it is. Looking at the world as a whole, Leibniz argued that, because one thing may be incompatible with or dependent upon another, a change in any one individual thing in the world would require that everything else be changed as well. In other words, there may be a number of possible worlds, in which things are quite different from those we find in this one, but within this particular world, everything has to be as it is. And, since he believed that it would have been possible for God to have created *any* sort of world, he argued that – since God chose to create this one – it must be *the best possible*. Two things follow from this:

Key thought

In other words (not those of Leibniz), freedom is not knowing all the reasons why you have to do what you do.

1 Within this world, we cannot predict exactly what will happen, since we do not have God's infinite mind and therefore cannot see the way everything works together. Therefore, not knowing that we are completely determined, we actually experience ourselves as free.
2 A world within which there is human free will, and in which there can be the evil and suffering that come from its misuse, is to be judged better than a world that lacks freedom but is free from its evils. He argued this on the grounds that a perfect God would create the best of all possible worlds.

Cross-reference

The second point here is sometimes referred to as 'the free-will defence' in discussion of the problem of evil. See *An Introduction to Philosophy and Ethics*, Chapter 4, section 1, and *The Philosophy of Religion*, Chapter 11.

But notice here that there is still a great difference between what is experienced (freedom) and what is actually the case (a world totally determined by the mind of God). How can these be related in such a way that the one does not undermine the other? This question was taken up again by Kant.

3 Kant: determined but free

Key question

How is it that, at one and the same time, I can appear to be determined, but yet know myself to be free?

One way out of this dilemma was given by Immanuel Kant in his *Critique of Pure Reason*.

He considered that the mind can understand phenomena by means of the concepts of space, time and causality. In other words,

Key words

Phenomena: things as we experience them.
Noumena: things as they are in themselves.

Key people

Immanuel Kant (1724–1804)
Kant was a thinker of the European Enlightenment tradition – seeking to get beyond authority and superstition and deal with the world on the basis of human reason. He argued that our knowledge of the world is structured by the way our minds organise our experience, rather than through direct knowledge of the way things are in themselves. His most important works were *The Critique of Pure Reason* (1781), *The Groundwork of the Metaphysics of Morals* (1785), *The Critique of Practical Reason* (1788), *The Critique of Judgement* (1790), *Religion within the Limits of Reason Alone* (1793), *Eternal Peace* (1795) and *The Metaphysics of Morals* (1797).

we do not say that everything has a cause because we have been able to check and identify a cause for each and every event (which would be impossible) but because our minds are so organised that they assume that everything they experience is an effect for which there has been a cause.

On the other hand, I know that I am free to choose and to act. I experience freedom, although, in the external phenomenal world, I cannot detect it. *Kant therefore saw the individual as phenomenally determined but noumenally free.* Everything I see in the external world is determined, but that is because of the way my mind works and perceives things, but I experience my own freedom – it is one of the presuppositions of every choice I make.

The implication of Kant's argument for the religious debate on this is that, rather than seeing some things as conditioned and others as free, it is possible to see everything as *both conditioned and free*. This has the added advantage of not letting human freedom get into a 'God-of-the-gaps problem' (see pages 75–76) where freedom is found only in the 'gaps' that have not been explained and cannot yet be predicted.

We should note also that both Leibniz and Kant wrote against the background of the seventeenth- and eighteenth-century approach to science, dominated by Newton. Their struggle is to understand how the Newtonian mechanism squares with the experience of freedom. However, the freedom–determinism issue has moved on from there, mainly because of new ways of approaching the role of religion, and also changes in the perception of science and in the way science has moved far beyond the narrow confines of the Newtonian world.

4 A Romantic challenge?

In the nineteenth century there was a move away from the mechanistic views of the seventeenth and eighteenth centuries, and a drive to experience nature in a more feeling, less abstract way. This is part of what is generally termed the 'Romantic movement', and it highlights the problems of trying to experience the world in the way in which science had described it.

'The stars,' she whispers, 'blindly run.'

This line, from Tennyson's poem 'In Memoriam', encapsulates the whole dilemma. If everything 'blindly runs', then the human body 'blindly runs', without freedom and without responsibility for its actions.

Of course, one way out of this was to seek a very different basis for religion. The theologian Schleiermacher described religion as

Key people

Friedrich Schleiermacher (1768–1834)
Schleiermacher was a Protestant theologian and philosopher, who worked as a university academic in Berlin and also had an active ministry as a preacher. He sought to justify Christian belief following the continental 'Enlightenment' (as represented by the work of Kant). His *On Religion: Speeches to its Cultured Despisers* (1799) was an attempt to show the deep personal and emotional roots of the religious impulse, and thus to present it as compatible with philosophy, science and culture.

'the sense and taste for the infinite', thus locating it very personally in the way in which human beings responded to life, rather than in the mechanistic world 'out there'. Religion could therefore retreat into being concerned with feelings and tastes, severing itself from the world of science.

Such reactions only served to confirm the gulf in people's minds between the 'objective' world and our 'subjective' experience of it. This can be expressed through various dualistic contrasts:

- Mind and body
- God and the universe
- Freedom and determinism
- Faith and reason
- Arts and sciences.

In each of these pairs, the first is based on a personal experience of, and relationship with, the world; the second is based on mechanical and physical theories which have been abstracted from experience, and by which experience is then interpreted.

The central dilemma of the freedom and determinism debate rests on the fact that we know we are free, but that as soon as we try to apply our abstracted theories to that freedom, it becomes part of a mechanical and determined system. The fundamental mistake here is in thinking that the mechanistic system, which informs me that I am determined, is somehow more 'real' than my own experience of freedom and choice.

5 Haeckel and Monod: a naturalistic view

Key thought

'Scientific materialism' is the attempt to show that all knowledge and reality are a product of the material world and depend upon its laws. It therefore dismisses morality and religion as the product of superstition, since it cannot be validated scientifically.

The temptations of scientific determinism

In 1899, Ernst Haeckel published *The Riddle of the Universe* (see page 28). He argued that everything, including thought, was the product of the material world and was absolutely controlled and determined by its laws. Freedom was an illusion and religion a superstition. He proposed what is generally termed 'scientific materialism', popularising Darwin's theory of evolution, and sweeping away all earlier philosophy which did not fit his naturalistic and scientific outlook.

On the other hand (as we shall see on pages 138–39) he did not deny that there was a 'soul' or self, rather he saw these things as natural phenomena, and as based on a material substratum. He was totally opposed to Descartes' dualism, with matter on one side and mind on the other. He is sometimes described as a materialist, but this is not strictly true (since it implies the non-existence of the world of thought, the self and freedom); what he actually claims is

Key quote

Haeckel claimed of his view that:

… it involves, on its positive side, the essential unity of the cosmos and the causal connection of all phenomena that come within its cognizance, but it also, in a negative way, marks the highest intellectual progress, in that it definitely rules out the three central dogmas of metaphysics – God, freedom and immortality. In assigning mechanical causes to phenomena everywhere, the law of substance comes into line with the universal law of causality.

THE RIDDLE OF THE UNIVERSE, 1899

Key questions

What would Haeckel have made of relativity and quantum theory? Would they have changed his views on the nature of determinism?

Key people

Jacques Monod (1910–76)
Monod, an eminent French evolutionary biologist, argued that evolution had no end point or goal, and did not see how a scientist could also claim to believe in God.

that all the 'spiritual' aspects of humanity arise out of and are dependent upon their material basis – and this he saw as a 'naturalistic' view of the universe.

His was also a 'monist' view: that there is one single reality, not two. Haeckel clearly believed that the doctrines of religion were based on superstition, encouraged by the notion of a dualistic universe in which mind or spirit was separated off from matter. He considered that, with further progress, science would lead to a unified system of thought that would explain absolutely everything.

It is clear, however, celebrating the end of a century of achievement in the sciences, that he felt that physics in particular had established itself beyond question and was now the dominant force in human understanding. It is interesting to reflect on the fact that the sort of physics he regarded as so soundly established was soon to be challenged by radical leaps forward.

But however much the scientific theories may have changed, the fundamental issue raised by Haeckel remained throughout the twentieth century: his form of scientific materialism basically considered science to be the only reliable route to knowledge, and matter to be the fundamental reality.

Jacques Monod explored the implications of molecular biology, and in particular the fact that evolutionary change is brought about by random mutations at the genetic level. He argued that everything that takes place at higher levels of organisation (e.g. for a human being) is ultimately the result of chance. Once the chance mutations have actually taken place, however, everything else follows from them of necessity. Chance and necessity between them therefore determine all that will happen. This view excludes any possibility of there being a God. In *Chance and Necessity* (1971) he claimed:

… pure chance, absolutely free but blind, is at the very root of the stupendous edifice of evolution.

and concluded by saying:

… man at last knows that he is alone in the unfeeling immensity of the universe, out of which he emerged only by chance.

Monod's assertion that emergence is 'only by chance' may be challenged. As Richard Dawkins and others have clearly pointed out, natural selection has the effect of taming chance, because it builds on successive positive steps. The evolution of any one species would seem to be neither rigidly necessary, nor pure chance, but a combination of the two, with chance mutations capitalising on their advantages, breeding, and thereby influencing the opportunities for future mutations.

Key thought

Monod's view of humankind's place within the universe, which sounds rather bleak and impersonal, has prompted other thinkers to develop the strong form of the 'anthropic principle' (see pages 69–70) in order to take a more positive and integrated view, seeing humankind's development as inevitable. However, this does not deny Monod's fundamental way of approaching the issue. Given chance initial parameters for the universe, necessity takes over and makes our present situation inevitable.

Now let us examine the implications of the ideas of Haeckel or Monod for the specific issue of freedom and determinism. Although as scientists they inhabited very different worlds, fundamentally they take the same position:

- Everything that happens depends on physical laws. Haeckel thought these could be determined; Monod (in the light of the twentieth-century advances in biology) sees the determined aspect of such physical laws as based on random, chance mutations.
- Neither of them will accept a dualistic universe where human freedom and thought stands over against a determined physical universe.

Monod was concerned to remove the idea of a creator God; the whole process of evolution was explained by chance and necessity. You do not need God in order to explain how the universe has come to be as it is. But the same argument can be applied to human freedom. To experience freedom and choice is to be creative – in a limited sense, it is to be god-like (and religion therefore makes much of the idea of freedom being given to humankind by God). Whatever I think I have freely chosen to do will (to follow the line of Monod's argument) be explicable in terms of chance (the particular circumstances and opportunities that were presented) and necessity (the laws of nature that, with hindsight, we can see as determining the choice that is made).

Between them, according to Monod, chance and necessity have provided an exhaustive account of what is experienced as free choice. But does that actually detract from my freedom?

Key thought

The crucial issue here is the extent to which science, in the predictions it makes, is able to claim that everything is determined by established laws, principles or statistical expectations, and whether that leaves any scope for freedom and choice.

6 Playing dice?

Key question

Is uncertainty predictable?

A characteristic feature of quantum physics is Heisenberg's 'uncertainty principle'. This states that it is possible to know either the position or the momentum of a particle, but not to know both accurately at the same time. In dealing with particles, it also appears that their behaviour is random – they are not 'caused' as are events on a larger scale. Hence, as we saw above (pages 55–56), quantum physics deals with probability rather than with individual certainty at the sub-atomic level.

It is sometimes argued that this uncertainty principle has revealed an element of chance or freedom at the heart of reality, and that this somehow allows for freedom rather than determinism at the level of human activity. But this is not justified. In quantum physics, simple events are undetermined – we cannot know what any one particle is going to do. What we do know, however, is what very large

Key quote

Quantum physics has nothing to do with the free-will problem.
E. SCHRÖDINGER, *SCIENCE AND HUMANISM*, 1952

Key thought

In terms of human behaviour, sociologists have recognised that there are general tendencies that behave rather like physical laws, but which are only known through statistics. In other words, they cannot show exactly how any one individual will behave, but they can predict with some accuracy how a percentage of people in a particular population are likely to behave.

We may be growing taller and/or wider, drinking more alcohol, using the internet more. These claims are based on statistical evidence, and remain true even if individuals go against the trend that the statistics reveal.

Key words

Reductionist: describes an approach that analyses complex entities into their component parts, with the view that reality lies with the parts rather than the whole.
Holistic: describes an approach, argument or view that considers the functioning of complex entities as a whole, rather than as the sum of their individual parts.

numbers of particles are likely to do. The quantum approach is therefore statistical.

Two things follow from this:

1 Nature can still be regular and predictable even if, at the sub-atomic level, individual particles are undetermined.
2 Therefore, at the level at which human freedom operates (or appears to operate), quantum indeterminacy is irrelevant. On the large scale, it is as unlikely that statistical probability will be overturned as that a 'law of nature' will be broken.

Einstein commented on the idea of indeterminacy by saying 'God does not play dice'. By this he meant that it is impossible to conceive of a universe in which everything happens in a random fashion. The whole of our ability to think and predict is based on the perception of regularity. Indeed, the whole success of the scientific endeavour is proof of the consistency of the phenomenal world. If things behaved in a random fashion, no science or technology would be possible, for they work by predicting and examining the results of predictions.

From the religious perspective it is also important to realise that two extremes are equally difficult to square with religion and morality: the absolute determinism of a mechanical universe, and the absolute freedom of a universe that operates in a totally random fashion. Randomness precludes any sense of meaning, purpose or value.

Reductionist and holistic approaches

There are two ways of examining any complex situation: by taking a reductionist approach or a holistic one. From a **reductionist** point of view, reality is found in the smallest component parts of any complex entity (e.g. you are 'nothing but' the molecules, atoms and sub-atomic particles of which you are comprised). If it can be shown that your constituent particles behave in a random fashion, then you, as a whole, are considered to be random, lacking any overall purpose. From a **holistic** point of view, reality is seen in the complex entity itself, rather than in its parts (e.g. there is something that is 'you' over and above the existence of all the separate molecules that make you up).

Generally speaking, reductionist approaches deny freedom, either by showing sub-atomic randomness (and therefore the lack of purposeful choice that freedom implies), or by denying any freedom of action by reducing everything to the mechanical rules that determine the operation of each component. Holistic approaches, by contrast, see freedom as a feature of complex systems.

Key thought

Freedom is a phenomenon of the present, determinism of the past. In other words, once a free choice has been made, it can be examined from the point of view of its circumstances and the motives that lie behind it. That process leads to the view that the choice was quite inevitable – and thus determined. *Looking back, we see reasons, and the world looks fixed; looking forward, we see choices, and the world looks free. In the present we experience a limited ability to make a difference; our world is plastic.*

The act of thinking and perceiving is one that involves a holistic approach. My eyes may scan and see a nose, a pair of eyes, hair, chin, clothes and so on. But my mind immediately puts those sensations together, checks them against memory, and experiences them together as comprising a particular person I know. Random perception would make nonsense of all human thought. You cannot think and encounter the world on the basis of randomness. For any science to make sense (as well as religion) there has to be the presupposition that the world itself makes sense, and for that there has to be some form of holistic view.

Summary diagram

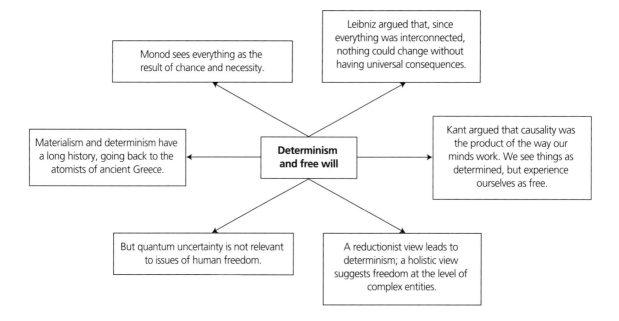

Monod sees everything as the result of chance and necessity.

Leibniz argued that, since everything was interconnected, nothing could change without having universal consequences.

Materialism and determinism have a long history, going back to the atomists of ancient Greece.

Determinism and free will

Kant argued that causality was the product of the way our minds work. We see things as determined, but experience ourselves as free.

But quantum uncertainty is not relevant to issues of human freedom.

A reductionist view leads to determinism; a holistic view suggests freedom at the level of complex entities.

Study guide

By the end of this chapter you should appreciate the fact that
science, because it shows causes and regularities and works towards a
complete explanation of things, tends to see everything as
'determined'. On the other hand, personal experience, religion and
morality work on the assumption of human freedom and choice.
The key question we have been considering is whether science
necessarily precludes freedom and whether religion necessarily
denies universal causality. Kant, Leibniz and others have sought to
reconcile the experience of freedom with the fact that everything
appears to follow the laws of nature.

Revision checklist

Can you explain ...?

- Kant's distinction between noumena and phenomena.
- Why Leibniz thought this was the best possible world.

Do you know ...?

- Why the Epicureans thought of the universe as impersonal.
- Why morality requires freedom.
- Why the 'uncertainty principle' may be seen as irrelevant to
  freedom at the human level.

Give arguments for and against ...

- The view that a total scientific explanation of an event
  excludes the possibility of human freedom.

Examples of essay questions

1. Is it possible for you to perceive my freedom? Discuss with reference to the philosophy of Kant.

AO1 This requires a clear statement about the distinction Kant
makes between the phenomena that we experience, and the
noumenal reality of things as they are in themselves. Clearly,
perception (of phenomena) cannot include freedom, since universal
causal determination is one of the ways in which our minds handle
and process the phenomena of experience.

AO2 This could explore what we mean by freedom, and whether
we can observe features of other people that we ascribe to their
experience of freedom, and whether we can use the analogy of our
own experienced freedom to impute it to others.

2. Leibniz argued that this must be the best possible world. If so, can you change any part of it without making it, on the whole, worse? Discuss.

AO1 This question invites a consideration of the interconnected nature of all phenomena, but also the sense that personal freedom implies the ability to choose and thus change the world.

AO2 In evaluating this, it would be appropriate to explore the question of whether it makes sense to speak of value in a materially determined universe, and thus whether a universe (or, indeed, a human action) could be described as 'better' or 'worse' than any other.

Further questions

1 Why is the idea of freedom necessary for religion and morality?

2 Do we arrive in this universe by chance?

9 MIRACLES

Chapter checklist

There is no clearer point of conflict between science and religion than the issue of miracles. The clarity of your understanding of this will influence how you see all other issues concerning religion and science.

1 Historical background

In the biblical world, events were not thought of as determined by fixed laws of nature, but open to spiritual influence. God was believed to uphold the natural order, and his will was seen especially in unusual events – signs and wonders, healings and exorcisms. The question asked was not 'How did that happen?' but 'What does it mean?' or 'Why did God choose to act in this way?'

However crudely the images of God may be presented (e.g. as someone who goes into battle, or stops the movement of the sun, to help his chosen people), the biblical view of God is certainly 'theism' rather than 'deism' – in other words, God is thought of as active within the world, not simply a detached, external creator, uninvolved with his creation.

The same view of an active and purposeful God is reflected in broadly based religious attitudes today. If a person asks 'Why should this happen to me?' when suddenly struck down by an illness, he or she is not really looking for an answer in terms of infections and immune systems. Rather, the quest is for some explanation which enables that person to make sense of the illness in the context of his or her life as a whole. For the believer in God, that amounts to asking why God has chosen that this should happen. Miracles were all part of this world view – a world in which certain events are interpreted as the result of God's direct action.

With the mechanistic explanation of the universe offered by Newtonian physics, the perception of miracles changed; they were

Key thought

At Fatima in Portugal, following reports by three children of visions of the Virgin Mary in fields outside the city, there were many reports of the sun spinning and zigzagging towards the Earth. It is now a holy site, receiving about 6 million visitors per year.

Clearly, both the visions and the accounts of the sun's movement might be termed miracles. But belief in such things is optional for Catholics, who are only required to accept those articles of faith that are based on the Old and New Testaments and contained in the Creeds. Nevertheless, the number of visitors alone shows that belief in miracles is still an important aspect of religion for many people.

seen as violations of the laws of nature. But since God was seen as the designer who had established the world on regular mathematical principles, miracles came to be seen by some as an unnecessary continuation of beliefs from a former unenlightened age of superstition rather than science. Thus, for example, Toland's book *Christianity not Mysterious* (1696) argued that Christianity should be stripped of its irrational elements, including its miracles.

Not all who saw God as a designer wanted to be rid of the miraculous. Newton himself accepted that God might intervene in the world, and William Paley (who re-formulated the design argument for the existence of God) saw miracles as proof of Christ's divinity (in his *Evidences of Christianity*, 1794).

We therefore need to consider three issues:

1 Can there ever be sufficient evidence to prove that a miracle (if this means a violation of a law of nature) has taken place?
2 Is it reasonable to accept miracles as part of a religious view of life?
3 How should accounts of miracles be understood, if they are to be more than simply violations of a law of nature?

2 Hume on evidence and miracles

Key question

If a miracle is defined as a violation of a law of nature, is it more likely that the accounts of miracles are mistaken than that the miracles actually took place?

David Hume pointed out that scientific laws were not true universal statements, but only summaries of what had been experienced so far. The very method used – gathering data and drawing general conclusions from it – yielded higher and higher degrees of probability, but there was no way of moving from this to absolute certainty.

Whether something should be believed or not therefore depended upon the strength of the evidence for or against it being true. It is illustrated by his approach to miracles, which he takes to be violations of a law of nature.

His argument, which clearly illustrates the empirical approach so central to the science of his day, comes in three parts:

1 On evidence:

A wise man … proportions his belief to the evidence. In such conclusions as are founded upon an infallible experience, he expects the event with the last degree of assurance, and regards his past experience as a full proof of the future existence of the event. In other cases he proceeds with more caution: He weighs the opposite experiments: He considers which side is supported by the greater number of experiments; to that side he inclines, with doubt and hesitation; and when at last he fixes his judgement, the evidence exceeds not what we properly call probability … A hundred instances or experiments on one side, and fifty on another, afford a doubtful expectation of any event; though a hundred uniform experiments, with only one that is contrary, reasonably beget a pretty strong degree of assurance.

2 On believing the testimony of others:

We frequently hesitate concerning the reports of others ... We entertain a suspicion concerning any matter of fact, when the witnesses contradict each other; when they are few, or of a doubtful character; when they have an interest in what they affirm; when they deliver their testimony with hesitation, or on the contrary, with too violent asseverations. There are many other particulars of the same kind which may diminish or destroy the force of any argument derived from human testimony.

3 On miracles:

A miracle is a violation of the laws of nature; and as a firm and unalterable experience has established these laws, the proof against a miracle, from the very nature of the fact, is as entire as any argument from experience can possibly be imagined ... The plain consequence is (and it is a general maxim worthy of our attention), 'That no testimony is ever sufficient to establish a miracle, unless the testimony be of such a kind that its falsehood would be more miraculous than the fact which it endeavours to establish;' ... When anyone tells me, that he saw a dead man restored to life, I immediately consider with myself, whether it be more probable, that this person should either deceive or be deceived, or that the fact, which he relates, should really have happened.

All three of these quotations are from his *An Enquiry into Human Understanding*.

His argument involved four steps:

1 To be a miracle an event must violate a law of nature.
2 To know if something has taken place, one must weigh evidence for and against.
3 Laws of nature are based on the maximum available evidence.
4 There can never be sufficient evidence to show that a miracle has taken place, since it will always be more likely (on empirical grounds) that a witness was mistaken than that a law of nature was broken.

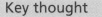

Key thought

This does not imply that a miracle *cannot* take place, simply *that there can never be sufficient evidence to show that it has*.

The Roman Catholic Church regards it as important to establish whether there is evidence to establish that a miracle has taken place. The Vatican's Congregation for the Causes of the Saints examines evidence for miracles, and a person can generally only be declared to be a saint (canonised) if miracles can be shown to have taken place as a result of requesting their help in prayer. Such examination involves the calling of witnesses and may take several years to complete. Therefore, whatever interpretations may be offered for the term 'miracle', the idea that it represents an event for which there is no natural explanation is still religiously significant.

3 Reasonably miraculous?

Key thoughts

Key thoughts

Strictly speaking, a 'violation of a law of nature' is impossible. You can violate a prescriptive law, simply by refusing to obey it; but how can you violate what is no more than a summary of your past action?

Science selects those features that are relevant and ignores the others. Thus, for example, you may watch an apple fall from a tree and thus become aware of gravity, but it is irrelevant whether the apple is green or red.

Scientific laws are *descriptive*, not *prescriptive*. In other words, the 'laws of nature' cannot in any way dictate what must happen; they merely summarise what has been found to happen in the past. Based on such summaries, of course (assuming that nature is uniform in the way it operates), it is possible to predict what will happen in exactly similar situations in the future.

If an event cannot be explained in terms of the existing 'laws', then the assumption is made that either our evidence for that event is incorrect, or that some other law is at work, and that this event is an example of that as-yet-unknown set of circumstances.

We have seen, for example, that relativity and quantum theory have shown that many of the principles of Newtonian physics are inadequate to deal with the cosmic or sub-atomic levels of reality. That has not overthrown Newton, nor has the action of sub-atomic particles been deemed miraculous. All that has happened is that Newtonian physics is shown to be valid only within a limited set of conditions, and cannot apply to the very large or very small scale.

It is also important to recognise that an event can be unique. In one sense, every event is unique, in that it takes place at a particular time and place and as a result of circumstances which will never be exactly the same again. On the other hand, science works by abstracting the most significant factors in each event, and making its predictions based on them – so that many events will be similar enough to one another to form the basis for a hypothesis.

Certain events are unique in the sense that they are found at extreme conditions that cannot be encountered more than once. The 'Big Bang' at the origin of the known universe is the most clear example of this. It can survive within a scientific theory about the origin of the universe, even though it cannot be compared with other 'Big Bangs' in other universes.

There are other situations – such as the 'event horizon' beyond which matter vanished into a 'black hole' due to the effect of extreme gravity – that are radically different from what can be found elsewhere in the universe. That does not stop scientists examining them, nor framing hypotheses relevant to them.

Therefore, in looking at the reasonableness of miracles from a scientific point of view, we need to be clear about the following:

- Science does not deny that an event can be unique.
- Science does not automatically rule out the possibility that an event may not be covered by existing 'laws of nature'.
- Science makes progress at exactly those points where existing theories fail to account for an occurrence. The task of science is to show the inadequacies of existing theories, and to frame better ones that take apparent anomalies into account.

Key thought

The crucial point is whether the interpretation offered for an event is reasonable given existing knowledge and the evidence available.

There is a general (and very wise) philosophical principle (known as Ockham's Razor) that, if there are two or more explanations for an event, you should always incline to the simplest or most straightforward. On this principle, the general criticism of any miraculous interpretation, from a scientific point of view, is that it does not represent the most *likely* explanation of an event.

4 Redefining the miraculous

Key thoughts

Not all modern thinkers try to redefine miracles. Richard Swinburne calls a miracle (in *The Existence of God*) a 'nonrepeatable exception to a law of nature'.

In 1988, samples of the material of the Turin Shroud (which was believed to bear the image of Jesus and to have been the cloth in which he was wrapped following the crucifixion) were taken for carbon dating at three separate laboratories in Tuscon, Oxford and Zurich. All three concluded that the Turin Shroud was a medieval forgery, dating from between 1260 and 1390.

That dating has been challenged, and may not be correct, but the shroud continues to be venerated and to be an object of fascination and enquiry to this day.

Another important issue for 'miracles' in the science and religion debate is what the direct action of God might mean in a world where all events are, in theory, capable of being given a scientific explanation. Can an event be called a miracle if it is also fully explicable in scientific terms? What is the significance of calling something a miracle?

It is possible, for example, to argue that accounts of miracles should not be taken literally. Here are three examples of this way of thinking:

- In 1670, Spinoza criticised the credulity of those who saw 'miracles' as evidence for the existence of God. He argued that the miracle stories in the Bible were not recorded to satisfy the reason, but to stimulate the religious imagination. They were *symbolic* rather than literal.
- In the nineteenth century, some theologians offered natural explanations for biblical miracles (e.g. Bahrdt's idea that Jesus might have been walking towards the boat on a huge submerged timber in John 6:12, rather than literally walking on water). Others (e.g. D. F. Strauss, *The Life of Jesus*, 1835) argued that miracle stories were *mythical*, literary devices, used in order to express the significance of Jesus, rather than describe what actually happened.
- The nineteenth-century philosopher Feuerbach saw accounts of miracles as projections of human desires – they described what people longed for, or thought should happen, rather than what did actually happen. In this sense they could be important emotionally and even religiously, but not factually.

Non-literal interpretations of miracles given by modern theologians tend to emphasise the significance of miracles in terms of *the values and qualities they depict, and the coded references found in them* (e.g. walking on the water and calming a storm might be taken in the context of ascribing divinity to Jesus, such things being a sign of acting with the power of the creator).

Key people

Ludwig Feuerbach (1804–72)
Feuerbach was particularly interested in religion, but came to the conclusion that God was a projection out onto the universe of all that was best in humankind. He thought that religion had much to contribute to a celebration of human life, and could best do so once shorn of belief in the external, objective existence of God.

Thus it can be argued that, even if it could be proved by overwhelming evidence that a man walked on water 2000 years ago, that action in itself, without further interpretation, would have no importance whatsoever. Only once the event is given an interpretation does it become significant.

5 Miracles and the arguments for the existence of God

Key question

Do 'miracles' undermine the traditional proofs for the existence of God?

Two important arguments for the existence of God depend upon a sense of the regularity and purposefulness of nature. The cosmological argument sees God as the uncaused cause or unmoved mover, providing an explanation for *all* movement or change. The teleological argument sees God as a designer, explaining why it is that things in this world work together in a way that appear difficult to account for in terms of blind chance. If nature were not predictable or purposeful, if events appeared haphazard or unrelated to one another, then the idea of a creator God would become problematic. How then does the idea of the miraculous relate to the idea that God is revealed through his handiwork in creating a predictable and purposeful universe?

For a theist, it is important that *everything* that happens is the will of God, and that nothing is outside his knowledge or control. That is the implication of the two central attributes of God – **omniscience** and **omnipotence**. But if that is the case, miracles would seem to be redundant; worse, they would be a sign of God becoming *inconsistent in his behaviour, changing his mind at whim.*

Key words

Omniscience: the quality of being all knowing (used of God).
Omnipotence: the quality of being all powerful; able to do anything (used of God).

This problem applies whether or not the concept of miracle is taken literally as 'a violation of a law of nature'. If it is literal, then God appears inconstant and the teleological and cosmological arguments lose their force. But if it is non-literal (in other words, if the term 'miracle' is used as an interpretation of an event which might otherwise be given a natural explanation), one needs to ask why a believer would ascribe significance to that one event rather than all others – for an omnipotent God should be responsible for all equally.

Richard Dawkins (in *Climbing Mount Improbable* and elsewhere) has argued that nature is indeed awesome and creative – the intricacies of life are to be wondered at, and the process by which they have developed is quite amazing. On the other hand, he sees no justification in going beyond that fact to posit the existence of a creator God.

Key thought

A small group of people, protected at the bottom of a stairwell during the collapse of the twin towers on 9/11, survived. But if their survival is called a miracle – as happened in a film made about their experience – does that not imply that an omnipotent God deliberately decided not to produce a miracle to save all the other victims of that attack? Does the concept of miracle not imply the unfairness of God?

Faced with that challenge, some believers might be tempted to call on special providence (see page 80) or miracles as a proof of

Key thought

The 'problem of evil' is another direct consequence of the concept of miracle. If God has determined that the world shall be such that it shall contain the possibilities of suffering and death on an appalling scale, then can he be 'good', or indeed, can he exist at all? The argument that in particular cases (miracles) the expected suffering is set aside points to a capricious God, and not one who can be thought of as a creator of the universe.

God's existence, by claiming that he shows himself in particular actions. But by doing so they have cut away the very basis of the theistic arguments, for by making God particular and his action localised, they have all but admitted that Dawkins is correct in finding the *general* creativity in the world is not in itself sufficient to prove a divine creator.

Summary diagram

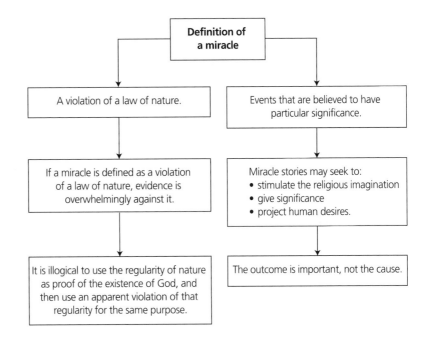

Study guide

By the end of this chapter you should understand Hume's argument against there ever being sufficient evidence to prove a miracle, and also be aware that accounts of miracles are concerned to show religious significance, not just to record events. You should also recognise that miracles continue to be important for many religious people, but that they conflict with some rational approaches to religious belief, including the cosmological argument for the existence of God and the argument from design.

Revision checklist

Can you explain ...?

- Why Hume was sceptical about all accounts of miracles.
- Why miracles tend to undermine some arguments for the existence of God.

Do you know ...?

- Why miracles raise questions about God's goodness and justice.
- What, other than uniqueness, is necessary for something to be called a miracle.

Give arguments for and against ...

- The view that religion needs miracles.

Examples of essay questions

1. Can there ever be sufficient evidence to prove that a miracle has taken place? Give your own views on the validity of Hume's argument and on his definition of what constitutes a miracle.

AO1 This requires an outline of Hume's presupposition that belief is proportional to evidence, and his definition of a miracle as a violation of a law of nature.

AO2 His argument may be challenged on two grounds: that his definition of a miracle is inadequate, or that he is wrong to say that one's belief should always be supported by evidence.

2. Is an interpretation of a miracle that does not involve the violation of a law of nature adequate for religious purposes?

AO1 This requires a clear grasp of those elements in the account of miracles – e.g. showing significance and value – that go beyond a violation of a law of nature.

AO2 This question gives students an opportunity to consider whether the language of meaning and significance is adequate for religious purposes if the event it purports to describe did not actually happen.

Further questions

1 Is the idea of a miracle incompatible with that of a God who knows and controls everything? Give your own views and your definition of what constitutes a miracle.

2 Is a miracle story shorn of its value once a natural explanation for the event it describes is found?

SCIENTIFIC EXPLANATIONS OF RELIGION

Chapter checklist ✓

Science examines phenomena and devises theories to explain them. But religion itself is a phenomenon – something that exists and may be examined – so we shall look at the explanations that science gives for religion's origin and continued existence.

1 Anthropological explanations

In 1841, the philosopher Feuerbach published *The Essence of Christianity*. In it, he argued that religion was essentially a human creation. It was a way of celebrating what is best in humankind, and did so by projecting those qualities out onto the universe. God was simply the best of humanity writ large.

He went on to argue that religious rituals were actually symbols that helped people come to terms with important aspects of life. Hence baptism, featuring a symbolic washing, was a way of expressing convictions about forgiveness and innocence.

Key thought

Following Feuerbach's theory, to worship God is really to affirm and celebrate those human qualities that he is said to display. In other words, to worship a God of love is to affirm love as the most important quality in human life.

Anthropology is the study of humankind. It tends to look at human societies and the various rituals and customs that they display. As anthropologists look at the phenomenon of religion, they see various degrees of sophistication and organisation:

- There is the basic religious awareness of the individual.
- There is the influence of holy people (or shamans), performing rituals and giving advice.
- There is the social aspect of religion, bringing societies together in celebration or to mark events in the life of the individual or society.
- There is also the more structured view of religions as large organisations with authority, doctrines and so on.

All of these can be examined from a human point of view. What the anthropologist explores is what the beliefs *do* for the people, what their function is within society. Whether those religious beliefs are *factually correct* is a secondary matter.

This approach may explain the function and continuing appeal of religion from three different points of view:

- Sociological explanations look at the way religion functions within society.
- Psychological explanations look at how religion relates to individual human emotions and needs.
- Biological explanations look at ways in which religion and morality may give individuals or societies an evolutionary advantage.

> **Key thought**
>
> These explanations of religion do not address the truth or otherwise of religious propositions. They simply examine why it is that people might be religious and what it does for them and their society.

2 Sociological explanations

Up until the eighteenth century, religion and science had appeared to offer their own particular interpretations of reality. Sometimes these coincided, sometimes they did not. It was only in the nineteenth century, however, that science turned its attention to religion, seeking to explain it as a human phenomenon.

Thus, as we look at the sciences of sociology and psychology, there are two very different things to consider:

- the compatibility of their views with those of religion
- their views on religion itself.

The issue to be debated in the second of these is not whether science can offer explanations that make the religious ones redundant, but whether science can explain the origins and continuing phenomena of religion itself.

> **Key people**
>
> **Karl Marx (1818–83)**
> Marx was an economic historian, a philosopher and a political activist. His research into social change led him to argue that class conflict was its driving force, and he argued for the inevitable failure of capitalism and its replacement by communism. He accused religion of offering bogus heavenly rewards to compensate for unfair conditions in this present life.

a) Marx

The basis of Marx's analysis of human society and the changes that come about within it is that human survival depends on the supply of food and other goods, and that the production and distribution of these create a network of social relationships. All other aspects of society (including religion) are shaped by this economic infrastructure.

His analysis of change in society was based on the idea of a 'dialectic', in which one thing (a thesis) produces an opposite reaction (its antithesis) and finally the two are resolved in a synthesis. Marx took this theory and applied it to the material base of society. His 'dialectical materialism' saw social change mainly in terms of the conflict between classes.

Key word

Alienation: a state in which people feel themselves to be deprived of personal achievement and satisfaction.

One feature of the capitalist society, according to Marx, is that working people suffer 'alienation' from nature, from their true selves and from one another. This was caused because they were required to work within a structure which detached them from the end product of their labours, and made them simply part of an impersonal capitalist enterprise.

His concern was to analyse society, criticise elements that led to alienation, and thereby encourage people – particularly the working class or proletariat – to take steps to overcome alienation and to free themselves from all that repressed them.

The Marxist critique of religion

Marx believed that religion encouraged alienation, because it offered illusory spiritual goals, which were held out by way of compensation to those who were suffering. These spiritual goals, he believed, took from people the incentive to actually do something here and now to improve their situation.

As such, religion was encouraged by those in power as a means of control. The spiritual rewards on offer provided an alternative to the material benefits that might have been theirs through revolution. Thus religion became a dangerous substitute for real progress.

Key quote

Religion is the sigh of the oppressed creature, the heart of a heartless world, the soul of the soulless environment. It is the opium of the people.
INTRODUCTION TO THE CRITIQUE OF
HEGEL'S PHILOSOPHY OF LAW

If religion survived through the longing of those who were oppressed, Marx argued that the way to overthrow it was not by arguing for atheism, but rather by means of a social revolution that would enable people to take responsibility for their own welfare and remove the causes of oppression. Once that was achieved, religion would no longer be needed and would therefore wither away.

Several key features emerge from this analysis:

- Religion is not neutral within society. It plays a part in the social structure within which it is practised, and its continuance may depend on that social structure rather than any truths that it may propound.
- As he saw it, religion had a negative and compensatory role, comforting those who were being oppressed. This may have reflected the situation of his day; it is a matter of debate whether that is a universal feature of religion.
- With social revolution and the achievement of real goals, he believed that religion would become unnecessary and wither away.

Key thoughts

- Notice particularly that Marx is not concerned with the *truth* of religion, but with the *function* of religion.
- Marx saw religion as a force opposing change. He had no concept of religion as a means of encouraging social justice.

In examining any phenomenon, science looks at what causes it and what maintains it. In a sense, Marx did that in terms of the needs of both the working classes (their longing) and those who oppress them (maintaining control by offering religion's substitute satisfactions).

Key thought

Pointing out the limitations of the data on which a theory is constructed is not unusual in science. In the light of relativity, Newtonian physics is seen as valid only within the narrow set of parameters. It does not mean that Marx's work is discredited – but, like all scientific theories, it should be open to revision as new evidence and perspectives become available. It would only be discredited if it refused to accept any new evidence that did not fit with its original theory – and that, of course, was the basis upon which Karl Popper criticised Marxism (see pages 38 and 39 for more on Popper).

Key people

Emile Durkheim (1858–1917)
Generally regarded as a major influence in founding the discipline of sociology, Durkheim taught at the Sorbonne in Paris. He claimed that the understanding of the phenomena of human societies must start with empirical observation, but also argued the society was shaped by moral values and the goals that people set themselves. He therefore saw religion in that context – as giving society purpose and solidarity.

Key quote

There can be no society which does not feel the need of upholding and reaffirming at regular intervals the collective ideas which make its unity and its personality.

THE ELEMENTARY FORMS OF RELIGIOUS LIFE

Social analysis, although very different from physics or biology, is a genuine form of science. Science is based on looking at phenomena and formulating hypotheses about them, which may be confirmed by further examination and experiment. That is precisely what Marx was doing, and his theories are to be accepted or rejected depending on the extent to which they continue to offer a rational explanation of the continuing phenomenon of religion.

One criticism of Marx's analysis, for example, is that many religious groups *promote* social action. How can they be accommodated in his theory? Another major criticism is that, with the emancipation of the proletariat, religion has *not* withered away, which suggests that it must serve a function other than that of offering illusory, substitute goals.

One may therefore see Marx as offering a valid set of theories for the particular social and religious situation of his day, but not as having produced a theory of universal relevance.

b) Durkheim

In *The Elementary Forms of Religious Life*, Durkheim argued that religion provided a framework of thought which is able to hold together the ideas and values that are shared by a society. Religion depends on there being a community of people who practise it; it is not about detached ideas and speculations. Particular religious beliefs may change, but the fundamental need for some sort of religion remains.

For Durkheim, religion performs the function of integrating and strengthening the group of people who practise it. Something becomes sacred because it is the means by which a group of people come to an overall understanding of themselves and their world. Thus for Durkheim, the real object of religious veneration is not a god, but society itself – for society and its need for cohesion is what lies behind religion.

Most sociologists today would agree with Durkheim that religion can express the values of society, and therefore that defending a particular religion is also a sign of social identity, but they would not try to go beyond that to say that society itself was in any way sacred.

c) Weber

Two features of Weber's sociology are of particular interest:

1 He emphasises the 'charisma' of religious leaders, who inspire their followers and pass on something of their own powers to them. Thus, in contrast to Durkheim, whose analysis of religion saw it primarily as a function of society as a whole, Weber saw it as a reflection of the potential and inspiration of individuals.

Key people

Max Weber (1864–1920)
Working in the universities of Berlin and Freiburg, Weber is generally regarded as the founder of the modern discipline of sociology. He was particularly interested in the impact on society of religious beliefs and moral views.

Key thought

Notice how this contrasts with Marx. For Marx it is the economic and social structures that give rise to and shape religion. For Weber, religion has an active part to play in the shaping of society.

Key people

Sigmund Freud (1856–1939)
Hugely influential as a result of his work on the unconscious mind and establishing psychoanalysis as a method of unlocking repressed experiences, Freud has changed the way people think about themselves, even where his specific ideas are challenged. He assessed religious beliefs and practices in terms of people's emotional and psychological needs.

2 He also took the important step of recognising that, in the relationship between religion and society, it was not just that society influenced religion, but that religion influenced society. So, for example, the Protestant ethic of hard work and personal frugality (as promoted particularly in Calvinism) contributed to the rise and success of capitalism.

Other sociologists have contributed views on the place of religion. Malinowski described the way in which religion deals with situations of emotional stress and trauma. Berger and Luckmann show the way in which it contributes to the overall framework of understanding and self-understanding, without which a society cannot hold together. Simmel examined acts of selfless devotion (e.g. of a parent for a child, or of a patriot for his or her nation) and showed the way in which these paralleled religious devotion. He thus saw these features of religion as universal human traits, without which society could not survive. *In general it is important to see that for sociologists what matters is how religion functions within society, not the truth content of religious beliefs.*

3 Psychological explanations

a) Freud

Jewish by birth, but not practising his religion, Freud spent most of his life in Vienna. After training in medicine, he worked as a hospital doctor, taking a particular interest in neuropathology and in the effects of the drug cocaine. He then set up in private practice, dealing with nervous conditions, especially hysteria, and developed a method of treatment called psychoanalysis. In this, through the analysis of dreams and by the free association of thoughts, a person could be led to articulate tensions which were previously locked within the unconscious mind, but which manifested in terms of bizarre behaviour or nervous or morbid mental states.

Freud is relevant to the study of religion and science for at least three reasons:

1 His theory about the unconscious mind raises questions about human nature, about whether we are actually free to choose what to think or feel, and about the image of God as father and creator. According to Freud, the mind is divided into the conscious, the pre-conscious, and the unconscious. Actions which a person may believe to be a matter of conscious choice may in fact be determined by unconscious influences, over which he or she has no control.

Key words

Conscious mind: includes those things of which we are aware.

Pre-conscious mind: includes those things that we may not be aware of at this moment, but which we are capable of remembering.

Unconscious mind: includes the memories of events that we are unable to remember, generally because they are too painful or embarrassing, especially events that took place in the earliest years of life, and which have therefore been repressed.

Key thought

Freud claimed that such neuroses could be cured if the sufferer was able to discover the root of the problem within his or her unconscious mind, as a result of which the tensions can be acknowledged and resolved. In other words, once a person sees that their feelings of dirtiness come from childhood and do not relate to their present state, they may be freed from their compulsive behaviour.

2 He claimed to give a scientific explanation of those personal aspects of life – motives, fears, hopes – which are seen as immediately relevant to the practice of religion.
3 He describes religion as an illusion, and offers a reductionist interpretation of its origins and continuing appeal. In other words, religion could be portrayed as a projection of realities that are actually to be found within the unconscious, which would tend to diminish its objective reality, whilst explaining its power over individuals and society.

Freud saw each stage of life as producing tensions. If these were not faced and resolved at the time, they could become buried in the unconscious, to re-appear later in life to create emotional or behavioural problems. He was particularly interested in neuroses which involved compulsive tidying routines or excessive washing. He ascribed these to feelings of uncleanness instilled in childhood. The adult is actually clean, but still feels dirty and therefore needs to wash. Such behaviour he called an 'obsessional neurosis'.

Freud saw in the meticulous observations of religious rites and duties a form of activity similar to the compulsive behaviour of his neurotic patients. He therefore believed religion to be a 'universal obsessional neurosis', motivated by unconscious guilt.

In *The Future of an Illusion* (1927) he set out various benefits of religion:

- that the threat from the impersonal forces of nature is handled by seeing them as controlled by a God. In other words, it is comforting to believe that whatever happens is the will of a loving God.
- that God takes the place of a human father, giving the adult the protection that a child looks for.
- that the believer hopes to influence events through the help of God, who rules the world.
- that there is a sense of dignity from having a relationship with God.
- that religion offers teaching that seeks to overcome the perceived threat of death.
- that religion gives a convenient explanation of otherwise inexplicable events.

But against these he sets the following arguments:

- that faith is actually an illusion, based on what people would like to be true, rather than what is actually the case.
- that divine rules and regulations may go against ordinary personal needs, thereby limiting personal growth.

There are many other interesting areas of Freud's analysis of religion, including his views on its origins, but for the purpose of the religion and science issues there are two crucial points to be made:

1   Freud showed that the motive for holding a religious belief may spring from personal and emotional need. Freud called religion an 'illusion' because he saw it as a projection of unconscious needs. On the other hand, it is important to recognise that this does not actually claim that religious beliefs are incorrect, i.e. God may exist, even if the reason for wanting to believe in him is the desire for a substitute father. So although Freud's argument may tend to undermine religious belief, it does not actually disprove it.
2   Crucial also for religion and science was Freud's claim that our actions are controlled by the unconscious mind. For him, beliefs and attitudes are not freely or rationally chosen, but are determined by experiences in our early childhood, buried in our unconscious. Again, this does not in itself refute any particular religious beliefs or moral convictions, but it tends to undermine any attempt to give them a metaphysical basis. They are, for Freud, a product of our unconscious mind.

The implication of Freud's position here is that, if religion is promoted because it fulfils emotional and psychological needs, then *the balanced and emotionally secure person does not need religion.* This is, of course, similar to Marx's idea that, once people recognise that their needs can be met in this life, they will not accept a substitute happiness in a future one.

Key people

Carl Jung (1875–1961)
Jung was a Swiss psychiatrist who diverged from the approach taken by Freud and founded the approach known as 'analytical psychology', and developed the concept of the collective unconscious. In terms of religion, Jung's work recognised the significance and function of mythology, art and culture.

b) Jung

Unlike Freud, who saw religion as an illusion hindering personal development, Jung gave it an important and positive role in human life. He claimed that all those people over the age of thirty-five who came to him with their problems were suffering from what finally amounted to a loss of the religious view of life. He remained agnostic about religious beliefs, whilst holding that religion itself had this positive part to play in human life. He accepted (following Feuerbach and Marx) that religious images were projections of the self, but then sought to show the importance that such projections could have in terms of the spiritual enrichment of human life.

As a scientist, Jung did not argue about whether or not God existed. He held that a person's knowledge is limited to those things which are experienced. His concern was to examine the idea of God in the mind of the believer and see how it worked. He also wanted to show that such ideas were found in all eras and cultures, and that they could have a positive, integrating effect.

Key thought

The collective unconscious and the archetypes
Jung introduced the idea of the *collective unconscious*. In this, an individual shares in a cluster of images (*archetypes*) found in different cultures and ages. Religion provides a rich source of these images, through which an individual is enabled to share in the cultural life of the whole race, and through which he or she can achieve a sense of personal integrity.

Two important points need to be kept in mind in assessing psychological or sociological theories of religion:

1 They reflect the experience of religion at a particular time and in a particular culture. In other words, if Freud's view of religion is one in which people are obsessed with guilt and forgiveness, his theories apply particularly to that aspect of religion. Such theories cannot apply to a religion like Buddhism, which includes neither guilt nor the concept of a 'father figure' god. Like all scientific hypotheses, they apply to a limited range of experience, and are open to revision.

2 They are a reminder that religion is not just a set of philosophical propositions, but a living experience. Psychological and sociological factors play a part in formulating and maintaining religious beliefs. The theories of Freud or Marx would suggest that those who do not have irrational feelings of guilt and unworthiness, or who do not look to an afterlife to compensate them for present suffering because they are in fact rather enjoying life just as it is, are less likely to be attracted by what religion has to offer. Whether that is in fact the case cannot be determined by a philosophical argument, but by observation of the actual pattern of religious belief in society today.

4 Biological explanations

Darwin himself argued that cooperation and altruism would give an evolutionary advantage, and in the animal world there are many examples of animals working to help one another. Wolves hunt in packs; some small fish whirl round in tightly packed shoals to protect themselves when attacked by larger predators. The extreme version of this is the ant or termite colony, where every activity is tightly structured and individual ants are given precise activities to carry out. You also see – even in reptiles – what amounts to kindly actions and social rituals that establish priority over a particular territory, or indicate a desire to mate, or an acceptance of a subservient position as a way of avoiding confrontation and conflict.

There is therefore a debate among scientists about the level at which natural selection works. It has been assumed that evolution progresses because advantageous genetic mutations are passed on from one generation to the next, and therefore that what counts is the benefit to close relatives – since they share much of one's own gene pool. This is the position popularised by Richard Dawkins. Natural selection takes place at the level of individual members of a species, who act as 'survival suits' for their genes, and those genes are passed on by breeding.

By contrast, Edward O. Wilson suggests that we should move to a new paradigm – group selection and colonies as 'superorganisms'. Ants provide a classic example of this, since ant colonies are constantly at war with one another, and what counts is the success and survival of the colony, within which individuals are prepared to disadvantage or sacrifice themselves for the benefit of the colony.

Wilson's approach is termed 'sociobiology'. It is the examination of social behaviour in the light of the Darwinian theory of evolution. Cooperation between members of a group is significant for its success, because it enables the group to benefit from the combined resources of its members (even if individual members have to sacrifice themselves in the process). Hence he argues that group selection is a more potent evolutionary force than individual or kin selection.

This, of course, has implications for an understanding of religion. In an article on Wilson by Bryan Appleyard (*The Sunday Times*, 23 December 2007), Wilson is quoted as saying:

> *Humans have an innate tendency to form religious belief. It has a lot of beneficial influences. It helps people adjust to their mortality and it binds communities tightly together ... to have evolved such a powerful tendency and to hold it unto death, that looks like a biological adaptation.*

Thus it is possible – given what sociologists have said about the significance of religion and morality within society – to see a biological advantage being given to those groups or societies that have developed moral or religious systems. Wilson himself, while remaining agnostic about religious beliefs, criticises Dawkins for being unscientific in his absolute opposition to religion.

In fact, the religious aspect of group selection is best explained in reverse – if there were not some biological advantage to be gained from religion, then religion would not be the persisting phenomenon that it is. In other words, anything which appears almost universally among the human species, and which emerges in different forms at different times and different places, and which then persists in spite of opposition, must be conferring some significant benefit – and hence may be a factor in group selection.

Notice that the main feature of the biological approach to the place of religion is – like the sociological and psychological approaches – less concerned with the truths of religious claims, but far more with the function of religion, both in terms of the individuals who take part in religious activities and also the effect of religion on society.

Key thought

Ants must have got something right – given that there are 10,000 trillion of them, as opposed to only 6.6 billion humans; that makes the collective weight of ants greater than that of humans!

Key people

E. O. Wilson (b. 1929)
In 1975, the evolutionary biologist Edward Wilson launched a new branch of study, which he called sociobiology – which was also the title of his controversial book. He thereby launched the modern debate about group selection. Previously, he had gone along with the prevailing orthodoxy, which saw natural selection at the level of individuals and close kin.

Key questions

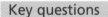

What do individuals, groups or societies gain from practising religion? Does it give them some advantage over others?

Summary diagram

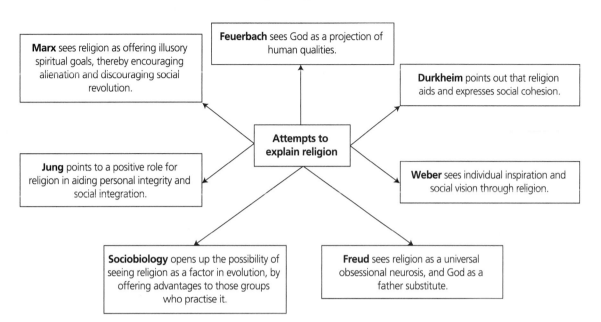

Marx sees religion as offering illusory spiritual goals, thereby encouraging alienation and discouraging social revolution.

Feuerbach sees God as a projection of human qualities.

Durkheim points out that religion aids and expresses social cohesion.

Attempts to explain religion

Jung points to a positive role for religion in aiding personal integrity and social integration.

Weber sees individual inspiration and social vision through religion.

Sociobiology opens up the possibility of seeing religion as a factor in evolution, by offering advantages to those groups who practise it.

Freud sees religion as a universal obsessional neurosis, and God as a father substitute.

Study guide

By the end of this chapter you should be aware of the ways in which the human sciences – anthropology, sociology and psychology – have examined religion as a human phenomenon, and also of the possibility that religion may persist because it offers an evolutionary advantage.

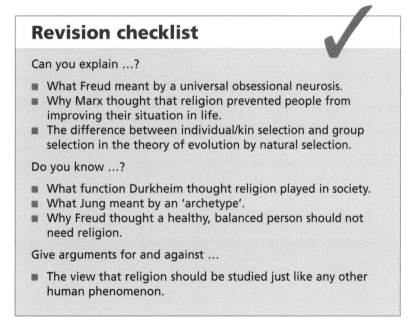

Revision checklist

Can you explain ...?

■ What Freud meant by a universal obsessional neurosis.
■ Why Marx thought that religion prevented people from improving their situation in life.
■ The difference between individual/kin selection and group selection in the theory of evolution by natural selection.

Do you know ...?

■ What function Durkheim thought religion played in society.
■ What Jung meant by an 'archetype'.
■ Why Freud thought a healthy, balanced person should not need religion.

Give arguments for and against ...

■ The view that religion should be studied just like any other human phenomenon.

Examples of essay questions

1. Do you consider the beliefs and attitudes of the Christian religion to be healthy from a personal and social point of view?

AO1 This question gives scope for an outline of the major psychological and sociological explanations of religion.

AO2 This requires an evaluation of whether religion is a prop, defending individuals against facing reality, or a natural expression of the values of a group. Some definition of what 'health' implies for humankind is required for a more developed answer.

2. If sociobiology can show that religion persists because it gives a group an evolutionary advantage, would that offer a positive endorsement of religion, or an adverse criticism?

AO1 This would require a basic outline of the idea of group selection, and an awareness of the sociological impact of religion.

AO2 You would need to consider whether true religion depends on the acceptance of supernatural beliefs, or whether the performance of religion for social reasons would be beneficial in itself.

Further questions

1 Comment on the following quotation from the standpoints of Freud and then of Jung, taking care to distinguish between them.

> [Many people] find it especially difficult to accept the objective or metaphysical side of religion, the side that postulates and describes various supernatural beings, powers and events. Though in many ways such beliefs are imaginatively attractive, we have little or no reason to think them true; they evidently belong to a bygone age, and they invite us back into a childhood world. The universe becomes again a vast family home in which we are destined to remain in perpetuity members of the younger generation under benevolent supervision.
>
> Yet although the doctrinal side of religion may thus seem hard to stomach and hard to credit, few people are happy to be quite without a religious dimension to their lives. At least they would like to retain something of a religious sense of life's meaning and something of religious ritual, values and spirituality.
>
> (Don Cupitt, *Taking Leave of God*, 1980)

2 Can you continue to believe in God, if you consider him to be a projection of all that is best in humankind?

11 WHAT IS A HUMAN BEING?

Chapter checklist ✓

Religions have much to say about people, their origins, their nature and their destiny. We therefore examine the scientific view of humankind, and see where it relates to the religious one.

There are two very different approaches to understanding what a human being is. In a *reductionist analysis*, complex entities are reduced to their component parts. Therefore, I am nothing more than the sum total of all the cells of which my body is made. Each of those cells is nothing more than the atoms of which it is composed. Each atom is nothing more than the sum of the particles, or quarks, of which it is comprised.

The analysis of objects in this way also implies that one branch of science can be reduced to another. Biology is concerned with living cells, but these can be reduced to the compounds of which they are made (chemistry) and finally to the atoms, which follow the laws of physics. In this way, although recognising that they have specialised interests in dealing with very complex entities, biology and chemistry are finally 'reduced' to physics.

The reductionist scientific analysis has a direct impact on issues we have already considered, such as freedom and determinism. I may experience freedom, but if the movement of every atom in my body is determined by physical laws, how is that freedom other than an illusion?

By contrast, a *holistic approach* does not reduce a complex entity to its constituent parts, but looks to see what the distinctive features of that entity are – features that can only appear because of its complexity. Holistic approaches recognise that different principles operate at different levels of complexity and identity.

What then is a human being? We can consider this question from these two different approaches: reductionist and holistic.

- From a reductionist point of view, as is often pointed out, a human being can be seen as forty-five litres of water, plus carbon, iron, phosphorous, fats, all organised harmoniously by the genetic code in the DNA. The human being is a marvel of complexity and organisation. Like jumbled pieces of a jigsaw puzzle in their box, you know that somehow all these molecules and atoms must fit together to form the single human image, but how they manage to do so is quite astounding.
- From the holistic point of view, a human being relates to others, thinks, chooses, wills, dreams, plans the future and suffers from events in the past. This complex entity exhibits a form of life that is of a different order from that of its constituent molecules.

Of course, these two ways of looking are not mutually exclusive. What happens at the level of individual cells can influence the whole person (e.g. when cells reproduce out of control and a life-threatening cancer develops). Equally, a holistic event (e.g. getting excited about something) has an immediate effect on many of the body's systems.

Clearly, religion functions at the holistic level. It is not concerned primarily with the way in which DNA controls particular cells, but with the behaviour and beliefs of human individuals and communities. In analysing what we mean by a human being, we will therefore need to keep a close eye on the balance between the reductionist and holistic approaches, ensuring that both are taken into proper consideration.

Key question

If human behaviour at the holistic level is controlled by and dependent on operations at the genetic or cellular level, does that render language about personal choice, morality and religion meaningless?

1 The place of human life

In the medieval world view, the Earth was central to the universe, and everything had a purpose related to human destiny. This followed the biblical view that God had created Man and given him authority over all other creatures.

Following the rise of modern science, it became increasingly clear that the universe was far larger than had been thought, and everything was seen as controlled by impersonal laws that had no relationship to human needs. Consequently the centrality of humankind was threatened.

Modern cosmologies have only heightened the awesomeness of the universe. Humankind may claim to have a significant role to play within the scheme of evolution on this planet, but when our solar system is lost among millions of others, the universe seems totally devoid of anything that could appear as providence or purpose related to humanity.

One of the functions of religious stories of creation was to 'place' humankind within the universe, giving to our species a sense of purpose. It is that basic function that is threatened by an impersonal universe in which humanity is located on a tiny, insignificant planet.

A sense of the insignificance of humankind is a valid religious response. In the book of Job, God silences Job's complaints by showing him the wonders of the natural world. Faced with such awesome sights, Job's demand that he be immune from suffering, or at least receive an explanation for it, utterly fails.

But DNA reveals something else – that the fundamental code for life is common to all living things. Through tracking the points at which the genetic code is held in common, we can look back to find common ancestors for presently diverging species. Ultimately, all living things share DNA – particular species have particular niches within the environment, some survive and multiply, others diminish and die out, but they are related. So humankind finds that its own sense of distinctiveness is blurred – it becomes simply one part of an on-going evolutionary process on Earth, a process in which it is bound up with all other species.

> ### Key thought
>
> This fact of the interconnectedness of all life is worthy of serious religious attention, and one that fits more naturally with Hindu and Buddhist thought than with the monotheistic religions, which have tended to emphasise the uniqueness of human life, for which other species are there in a subsidiary role, or to provide nourishment.

2 Human origins

In the nineteenth century, as we saw, the theory of evolution was a key feature of the debate between religion and science, with Darwin's natural selection seen as a threat not only to the creativity of God but also to the place of humankind within the natural order. With the appreciation of genetics, the balance has shifted somewhat by the overall recognition that the genetic make-up of humans is not that different from the other species to which they are closely related, and that – whatever their origins – they are well integrated into the web of life that embraces all species. Thinking of humankind as a separate and very different species, added to an existing world of plants and animals, is simply to go against the fundamental insights of modern biology.

Another feature of genetics, applied to human origins, shows that the idea of humankind starting with a single original couple, Adam and Eve (an idea termed *monogenism*, or the *Adamic theory*), is very improbable. For this to have taken place would require a mutant couple (i.e. a pair sharing exactly the same mutations) who were also sufficiently different from the rest of their species to prevent interbreeding. Whereas the more normal way for a new species to become established is for the gradual accumulation of differences in one group to separate them off from the rest of their species, as sometimes happens through geographical separation. So, once again, in its origins, humankind is shown to be integrated into a wider process of evolution and change.

It is also valuable to reflect on the relative age of the human species, compared with that of the Earth, which, at about 4.5 billion years, is about one-third of the age of the universe itself. Key features of the development of life on Earth would include:

- Vegetation and dry land: 410 million years ago.
- Major destructions of existing species: 250 million years ago (approx. ninety per cent of species destroyed) and 65 million years ago (the dinosaurs, who had dominated the Earth for about 165 million years, and approx. fifty per cent of other species destroyed).
- Mammals appear: 50 million years ago.
- First apes: 35 million years ago.
- *Australopithecus*, an early hominid: 4 million years ago (brain capacity increases from 450 to 750 cc).
- Hominid remains found in north-western Spain, dating back between 1.1 and 1.2 million years, are thought to be the ancestor of both *Homo sapiens* and the Neanderthals – they were found with stone tools and chippings and the remains of animals which suggest that they were meat eaters. These are the oldest remains to be found within Europe. By 700,000 years ago, *Homo erectus* is found in Africa, Asia and Europe (brain capacity increasing from 800 to 1200 cc).
- Neanderthal remains found in Europe dating back 300,000 years.
- Three well-preserved skulls, found in Ethiopia, date back 160,000 years and are therefore thought to be the earliest fossils of *Homo sapiens* (although a date of 195,000 years has also been claimed for this). And that date corresponds to the age at which *Homo sapiens* is thought to have diverged from other hominid species, as calculated by the analysis of human DNA. This also shows that *Homo sapiens* is not descended through the Neanderthals, who were a separate hominid branch, finally dying out about 32,000 years ago.
- Genetics has enabled us to estimate that the whole of the present human race has come from an original group of about 10,000, living between 100,000 and 150,000 years ago.

By the time you get to 40,000 years ago, with a brain size at 1400 cc (much the same as that of modern man), you find paintings and language, and then – about 10,000 years ago – there are the first settlements in the Fertile Crescent of the Middle East.

Key thought

Some branches of this tree have lived on in particular parts of the world. Remains of a very small 'hobbit' form of humans have been found on the island of Flores in Indonesia, having lived there until about 13,000 years ago. How does awareness of such relatives of modern humans influence a religious understanding of the place of humankind in the scheme of things?

Key thought

Whatever questions are raised about human origins, the figures given above (which are very approximate and are open to scientific challenge and revision) at least put the very brief period of time during which human beings have lived on Earth into some sort of perspective.

Consider, then, what long periods of apparently slow development come before a newly defined stage in human development is reached. Modern man is a very recent phenomenon – but so is all life, compared with the age of our planet!

As we saw above, a creationist approach would see humankind as a special creation of God, set within a young world that was created to provide for its needs. The question remains whether one can see the scientific view as diminishing humankind – by showing its slow development and links with other species – or whether in its own way this whole sweep of evolution and development is a positive affirmation of the specialness of humankind (just as any species in its own way is unique and special).

3 A human machine?

Key people

Galen (c.129–216 CE)
Born in the Greek city of Paramus, Turkey, Galen started to study anatomy by examining the corpses of animals, but also gained experience in human anatomy and the treating of trauma wounds by working as the physician to a gladiator school.

The Roman physician Galen thought that the purpose of the heart was to create heat, and that air from the lungs stopped the body overheating. Blood was drawn into the right side of the heart, seeped through to the left, was purified, mixed with vital spirits, and then moved off into the arteries. Such was the influence of Galen that Vesalius (1514–64) (in *De Fabrica*, 1538), a physician who is regarded as the founder of the study of anatomy, falsified his own findings in order to make his view of the workings of the body correspond to that of Galen. Nevertheless, it was when this view was challenged by Harvey (*De Motu Cordis*, 1628), who – following nine years of experiments – established that the heart was a pump, and that blood was oxygenated in the lungs before being pumped through the body, that real progress was made in analysing the workings of the human body.

It was realised that each organ was nourished by oxygenated blood and the whole body seen as an interconnected system. Individual organs lived because the body as a whole incorporated a system for delivering to them what they needed.

Compare this view with the traditional one of Western religions. In Genesis, man is made out of dust (*adamah*) and becomes a living soul (*nephesh*) through receiving the breath of God. A person is therefore fundamentally an animated body, and once God's breath is removed, that person returns to the dust from which he or she was made.

Greek thought went a stage further. Plato thought that a human being comprised an eternal soul (which existed before birth, and would survive death) linked to a physical body. The distinction was

Key thought

Christianity combined the Hebrew sense of humankind being alive with God's breath, with the distinctions made in Greek thought. The mind and the soul, although linked with the body here on Earth, were the bearers of its spiritual destiny. Those who live according to the spirit are contrasted with those whose life is based on the flesh.

Key thoughts

What is clear is that the elements in human experience that religion features are those that take a *holistic* view – they are to do with *the person* and his or her response to life. This need not deny any of the results of analysing the body into its constituent parts, but claims that such analysis and genetic functioning are *not the whole of what human life is about*.

The human being is the product of genetic code – but that does not make it *the same thing as* genetic code, just as the journeys made in a car cannot be equated with the parts of which the car is built. It makes no sense to deny the validity of discussing the purpose of road transport just because I have discovered that it all depends on the workings of the internal combustion engine!

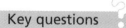

Key word

Intentionality: an approach to speaking about the way in which people act and interact with their environment. They choose to do things based on their beliefs, desires and hopes; they frame intentions to act. Their action is not to be explained adequately in terms of muscles and electrical impulses that are involved. It includes those things, of course, but it is best explained with reference to my original aim or desire.

Key questions

Why is it that the human machine has intentionality? Why does it hope for things, seek out goals, and choose what to do? Can the analysis of the body ever show that intentional stance?

made between the physical flesh (*sarx*) which made up the human body (*soma*), which possessed natural life (*psyche*), a thinking element (*nous*) and a spirit (*pneuma*).

The important thing to recognise from all this is that, from a religious point of view, if human beings are to have those things that seem basic to religion – freedom, morality, the spiritual life, the ability to respond to God – they must be considered as 'more than' simply the physical, mechanical body, however complex and awesome its organisation may be.

Our knowledge of the *human genome*, the sequence of genes strung out along the human DNA, has led to a closer awareness of the way in which humans relate to other species. Although the genes that control the production of human proteins differ from those of other species, we all have about the same number of them – simpler forms of life tend to have different genes, not fewer genes.

The genome goes beyond the division between reductionist and holistic approaches to understanding a human being. On the one hand, to say that the design of a human being is controlled by a sequence of nucleotides in the genes is to suggest reductionism – we are 'nothing but' what our genes determine we shall be. On the other hand, the sophistication and sheer complexity of DNA, and the ability of the human body to spot where something is going wrong and to correct it (a feature of the body's immune system), suggest that the whole works to police and act upon the parts. We are not totally at the mercy of the reproduction of individual cells – for the role of every cell is clearly defined and controlled.

Notice also that the genes are not like individual persons who can act intentionally. When Richard Dawkins wrote *The Selfish Gene*, he was concerned to show that selfishness – in the sense of wanting to reproduce and maximise one's own future chances – was a feature of one's genes, not of individuals. And genes, of course, are not morally responsible entities.

To sum up, you can analyse the body and show the workings of its various parts, just as you could analyse a machine. That shows its complexity and the way in which all the parts work together in order for a human being to function. What it does not show is anything to do with the *experience of being human*. In other words, it cannot account for morality or social relations, or beliefs or ideas. If it is a machine, then the human machine has gained *intentionality* – and that makes it very different from machines that are contrived by humans, because they are given their purpose by their human creators.

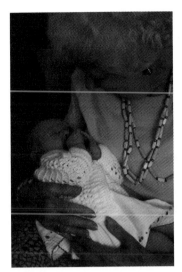

Eighty-seven years separate this baby from her great-grandmother. How is personal identity maintained over all that time? How can this baby be identified with the elderly person she will one day become?

Religion deals with people, not machines. It speaks of individuals and their destiny, of what they value and of the purpose of their lives. That tends to assume that a person has a fixed identity, given at birth (or perhaps at conception) and lasting through until death, and – for those who believe in it – a life beyond death.

But in looking at the human anatomy (and, in the next section, also the human brain), it is difficult to identify exactly what (if anything) constitutes that fixed 'person'. During life every part of the body is changed and renewed. What gives continuity between a baby and the adult into which he or she will one day grow? Is it possible to think of some separate 'soul' that is constant, while the body changes?

Science reveals a human being as a set of interlocking biological systems, the product of a long period of evolution, each individual built according to instructions coded in their DNA. Does that enhance the wonder at the phenomenon of human life, or make it more difficult to believe in the idea of human individuality?

4 Minds, brains and artificial intelligence

Key question

If it were possible to reproduce the brain artificially, how would such artificial intelligence relate to the idea of a person, self or soul?

The human brain is the most complex entity known. It consists of about 10^{10} long nerve cells, each connecting with about 10,000 similar cells, their interfaces controlled by chemical messengers. But, however complex and however central to the control of everything in life, the brain is simply one part of the human body, and it is not what religion or philosophy terms the 'soul', 'self' or 'mind'.

Naturally, brain activity is closely linked to thought – so that, for example, if someone suffers brain damage that is likely to affect their ability to think. But that does not mean that we can simply identify the process of thinking with the activity in the brain – for that would be to make a *reductionist* analysis that would hardly do justice to the experience of thought (any more than a huge printout of digits would be a substitute for the music I hear on my CD, even though I know that the CD is actually no more than a way of communicating that sequence of digits).

From all that we have considered so far, it is clear that the sort of human activity with which religion is concerned – thinking, choosing, valuing, celebrating, sympathising, worshipping – is not easily recognised once it has been through a process of reductionist analysis. It would simply become sequences of electrical impulses within parts of the brain; but that's not at all that those things mean for people.

Key thoughts

Your brain is a power-hungry organ, consuming about a quarter of your oxygen supply and much of the energy generated by the food you eat. It is estimated that half of all your 25,000 or so genes are dedicated to the production of the brain. Electrical and chemical messages flow within the brain and between the brain and all other organs – and we know which parts of the brain control sight, speech, memory and so on. Even if computers can simulate brain functions, the quantitative difference in terms of complexity is immense. That complexity gives the appearance of simplicity – since the brain is just soft grey material, rather than banks of microchips – and the sophistication of its operation, since it is perfectly natural for us, is therefore hidden.

The brain may integrate and process all the stimuli that we receive, it may control what we think and do, we may even identify which parts of the brain control particular human skills and attitudes; but that does not identify the brain with the 'self' any more than a drive in the countryside can be identified with the workings of the car we use.

I may accept, for example, that a chimpanzee shares ninety-nine per cent of its genetic material with a human being, and at that level they are very similar creatures. On the other hand, when it comes to matters of philosophy, religion and ethics, the species appear to be utterly different; the chimpanzee lacks those very distinctive human qualities and abilities which make reflective thought and religion possible. The reason for this difference between humans and their close genetic neighbours may lie in brain capacity: 400 cc for the chimp compared with the human 1400 cc.

But it is probably not simply a matter of brains, for we know that people's behaviour and attitude can change as a result of a whole variety of things – the environment within which they live, the food and drink they consume, the various stimuli they receive. Emotions are as much about chemistry as they are about electrical activity in the brain. In other words we need to recognise that the brain is simply one part of a set of physical connections that link us with the rest of the universe.

The dilemma is how you identify the 'self', if it is neither the brain, nor any other part of the physical body. And this is a problem for religion in its encounter with science. For example, in 1950 the Roman Catholic Church issued an official statement on evolution (*Humani Generis*) in which it stated that evolution could be discussed as a hypothesis about the development of the physical human body, but that the soul is immediately created by God. This implies a dualism of body and soul, as represented by philosophers like Plato or Descartes. And this, of course, is important for any religion that wants to claim that people in some way survive death; there needs to be something that can remain untouched by the physical dissolution of the body.

It is possible, of course, that the mind or soul is simply another, very subtle part of nature. At the end of the nineteenth century, Haeckel, in trying to show that science was able to vanquish superstition and religion, did not try to deny that there was a 'soul' or that morality was possible, but argued that what people called 'soul' was a natural phenomenon. He was against any idea of a separate realm of the spiritual:

This hypothetical 'spirit world,' which is supposed to be entirely independent of the material universe, and on the assumption of which the whole artificial structure of the dualistic system is based, is purely a product of the poetic imagination; the same must be said of the parallel belief in the 'immortality of the soul,' the scientific impossibility of which we must prove more fully later on. …

Our own naturalistic conception of the psychic activity sees in it a group of vital phenomena which are dependent on a definite material substratum, like all other phenomena …

… like all other natural phenomena, the psychic processes are subject to the supreme, all-ruling law of substance …

(*The Riddle of the Universe*)

A great deal has happened in science since Haeckel's day, and a present-day scientist is likely to speak about these things rather differently. But there is one element in his argument that remains relevant: he points out that psychic activity depends on a 'definite material substratum'. Is it possible, therefore, in constructing an appropriate 'material substratum', to produce psychic activity – in other words, can you build something that takes on human qualities and characteristics?

This brings us to the issue of artificial intelligence. The more complex something is, the more personal and spontaneous it appears. Early computers were very crude; they processed sets of instructions in a methodical way, but not one that appeared in any way to display creativity. But increase memory and processor speed and the interaction between the operator and the computer starts to become more like the interaction between two individuals – the computer appears to take on an intelligent life of its own.

On the one hand, it becomes increasingly difficult to define exactly what it is that computers cannot do that would be necessary for them to be considered to be thinking and relating in a human way. Equally, it is clear that a computer is only as good as the information programmed into it, and that programming depends on human beings.

But this should not allow human beings to remain smug, for they too are programmed. The whole world of language and thought, whatever our latent disposition to develop it, is something that we are taught. Our language and ideas do not arrive in our heads from nowhere – they are a response to our human environment. Is this so very different from the process whereby a computer is programmed?

If intelligence is considered in a functionalist way, it is simply a matter of receiving inputs, processing data and providing outputs. Take a very simple example: a child puts his or her hand near something hot, feels a burning sensation and quickly withdraws it. The input is the feeling of burning, the processing of the brain registers this as unpleasant and computes that moving the arm away will solve the problem, and the output is the instruction to the arm muscles. Of course, all that happens in a fraction of a second and is instinctive. But in theory it is the sort of process that could be carried out by a computer.

As computers become increasingly sophisticated, they can learn from experience and can 'think' in a way that reflects human thought. But what does that say about human beings?

Key thought

The computer can be seen as no more than a mechanical tool (albeit a very clever one) that can reflect back the intelligence and personality of its human creators.

- Are we no more than elaborate computers?
- Or, to take the other side of that question – should computers be regarded as individuals? If so, should they be given rights, treated morally and so on?

At one time it was fashionable to see animals as little more than organic machines, with no rights and no expectation that we should care for them. The human species alone had a privileged position in nature, along with rights and obligations. We now regard that as inadequate when it comes to assessing how to treat, say, one of the higher apes. They are so sufficiently like us, and so able to communicate their distress if hurt, that we tend to say that they should be treated with appropriate respect.

How then, on a scale that runs from a simply computing machine, through sophisticated computers, through animal brains and up to humankind, do you decide where – if anywhere – you are going to put the division between those who count as persons and those who do not?

Persinger's helmet

A Canadian neurologist, Michael Persinger, has worked on the question of how the human brain responds when placed within complex magnetic fields. Many who have submitted themselves to his helmet, set up in a carefully controlled environment, have experienced things that might be described as 'religious' in the broad sense, including a sense of being in the presence of some higher being, or a sudden sense of creativity and inspiration.

The key question for the religion and science debate is exactly what this can show. If magnetic fields can set up experiences that seem religious, does that invalidate religious experiences, or does it simply demonstrate the physical aspect of an experience that is valid in itself, irrespective of its origin?

It also comes down to where you stand on the issue of a separate, independently acting God. If God can only act where there is no physical explanation (as in the traditional sense of a miracle being a violation of a law of nature), then Persinger's helmet might suggest that God can be eliminated; religion is really no more than a sensitivity to magnetic fields. On the other hand, a conventional theistic view sees God as acting within the world, therefore there seems no reason why a theist cannot accept that similar experiences are produced by magnetic fields – on the grounds that they might be no more than the instrument that God chooses to use. On the other hand, it does suggest that religion is a *natural* phenomenon – explicable like any other – and that is something that many religious people are reluctant to accept.

Key word

Neurotheology: not a scientific term, but one that refers to the study of brain activity associated with religious experience.

Persinger's work is just one example of what Aldous Huxley, the novelist, termed **neurotheology** – the study of the neurological aspects of religious experience. We already know that alcohol, drugs and electroconvulsive therapy can change the way people think and perceive the world. We also know that damage to particular parts of the brain directly affect various aspects of mental function. It is therefore quite understandable that the phenomenon of religion and religious experience will have a neurological component – indeed, it would be remarkable if it did not, since everything else we do in our physical and mental life has a direct link with brain activity.

The key question remains, therefore, as to whether the recognition that religion has such a link with brain activity actually matters or makes any difference either to science's view of religion or religion's view of science.

Key thought

If religious experience is related to specific areas of brain activity, one cannot argue that religion does not exist. But it is possible to say that religion is *no more than* such brain activity. However, the fact that my sense of taste is related to activity in the cerebral cortex does not mean that my enjoyment of food is lessened.

You may tell me that the gustatory receptors in the papillae on my tongue are stimulated by chemicals in my food, and that the resulting electrical messages are disentangled within the cerebral cortex to give the experience of taste, but that does not lessen the enjoyment of my apple. The benefits of religious experience may not be lessened, therefore, by being linked to brain activity.

Many things we do are in response to emotions – fear, anger, excitement and so on – indeed, it can be argued that our survival depends on knowing whether to fight or run away when threatened. The negative feelings, stimulated by external threats, are controlled by a small part of the brain called the amygdala. At one time, doctors operated on the amygdala experimentally, in the hope of being able to control patients with violent reactions. Now it is known that the amygdala handles a whole range of negative emotions, including sadness and a sense of disgust.

Here you have a direct correlation between a small part of the brain, and a very personal range of negative emotions and responses. Brain activity in the amygdala corresponds to some very significant attitudes to life, and also to our moral sense. Some philosophers (e.g. David Hume) have argued that morality stems from a basic sense of revulsion at the sufferings of others, leading to altruism – and we know that such revulsion is related to this particular bit of brain matter.

Even more significant are the frontal lobes of the brain's cortex. This is the area that is involved with self-control, and controlling social behaviour. Of course, none of this suggests that neurotheology ought simply to equate religion and morality with bits of brain activity, but it does show that the brain has a range of functions, and is not just processing information from the senses. It is deeply involved with the world of feelings and responses.

Indeed, a functionalist analysis of the brain shows that it first receives data from the senses, and then sorts out how it should respond; in other words, it has an input, a sorting process and an output.

Daniel Dennett (in *Kinds of Minds*, 1996, and other books) argues that having a mind is a matter of being guided by representations. In other words, we do not just experience things, but we are self-conscious in taking a view about those things and deciding how we are to respond to them.

Minds, therefore, are not about brain activity, but about the concepts and representations that we use in order to make our choices in life. They do not exist *apart from* brain activity, but speaking of them is certainly *not the same thing* as speaking about brain activity. Where does religion stand in relation to this?

Well, concepts such as 'God' or 'the self' or even an interpretation of an experience as 'the holy' are *mental representations* that guide subsequent interpretation of experience. They are no more and no less physical than any other mental representations. Hence, it is perfectly valid to explore their meaning and significance, quite apart from any discussion about whether they refer to things that *actually* exist externally to us.

God can be a regulative mental concept, gathering together a sense of who we are and of our place in the universe; it may give a sense of peace and integrity. As such it has a positive value for the individual who uses it, quite apart from any question about whether God literally exists. The concept 'God' does something, and that forms the basis of religion.

Key word

Functionalism: at its simplest, a functionalist view of the mind looks at the process by which the brain receives data, assesses it and then decides what the body should do in response. The mind is not simply a data store, but a way of developing and acting on beliefs, based on experience. It acts a bit like a computer program, sorting and processing inputs and generating outputs.

Key question

What role does religion play in the functionalist analysis of mind? (In other words, given people's experience of the world, their responses to it – including both their feelings and their actions – in what way does religion influence that process of learning, deciding and acting?)

5 Surviving death?

In this section we shall look at the idea of immortality, the Christian doctrine of resurrection and theories of reincarnation and re-becoming, for these need to be explored in the light of what science tells us about a human being.

Human **immortality** depends upon identifying something that transcends the changes of our material environment – for everything that we see and know in this world is contingent (in other words, there was a time when it did not exist in its present form).

Key words

Immortality: the belief that part of a human being (generally described as the essential self or soul) does not die with the physical body.

Resurrection: the belief that, after death, God raises human beings to life at the end of the world, when they are judged and either rewarded or punished.

Reincarnation: the belief that a self or soul can pass on to another body after death.

Re-becoming: the Buddhist view that human beings, like all complex entities, are constantly changing, and that there is no fixed self.

Key thoughts

Modern cosmology opens up the most amazing vistas, in which energy is transformed into matter, and matter is changed again and again. Thus, the very elements of which we are made were forged in the nuclear reactions within a dying star. Every atom of your body pre-dates the present solar system; you are using them on a very temporary basis. What are the implications of this for some traditional beliefs about mortality and immortality?

A human being is more a process than a thing – it is a network of constantly changing systems.

Immortality cannot depend on our physical existence, for that is extremely temporary. Nor would it make sense to try to identify personal immortality with the fundamental energy of the universe – for that would be to lose all sense of personal identity. The physical re-constitution of a physical body after death is also rather a curious notion, in the light of the way in which the body is constantly changing anyway.

The main arguments for immortality have traditionally been based on the nature of thought.

- Plato, contrasting particular objects with the ideal 'forms' of which they are examples, believed that we have some innate knowledge of these 'forms' and that such knowledge must have been acquired before birth.
- Descartes, in his systematic attempt to doubt everything, concluded 'I think, therefore I am' on the grounds that he could not doubt his own thought. This led to a radical dualism, with matter on one side and mind on the other.

The dilemma with such beliefs is to identify what it is that could survive:

- Is a disembodied existence possible?
- If so, what would it be like?
- Can you have a personality, or even a thought, if you have no body?
- What would it mean to survive in a non-physical sense?

Of course, such questions are very different from those that one might ask of the traditional Christian concept of life beyond death, which (contrary to popular opinion) is *not* about immortality but about **resurrection**. Christian belief is that human beings do not possess their own immortality, but receive it from God, who raises them up from death. This is central to the Christian view of Jesus' death and resurrection. It is not that there was a bit of Jesus (his mind?) that somehow survived crucifixion; rather, Christians believe that Jesus did actually die, but that God subsequently raised him up. In the same way, they believe that, after death, they will be raised up and given a new body. This at least acknowledges the idea that in order to live you need to have a body. The problem is to know how such a new body might be thought of, especially since it cannot be part of the existing world – for that would simply be the re-assembly of existing atoms.

Some Eastern religions take a very different view. The concept of **reincarnation** allows a 'self' to move from body to body – this allows the idea of a self that is not simply identified with its physical body, whilst at the same time acknowledging that it is difficult to see how a self or soul could be said to live on without some sort of body as a vehicle for its self-expression. But reincarnation of this sort still depends on a radical body–soul or body–mind dualism.

The only radical religious alternative to this is given in Buddhist thought where everything is in a radical state of change from moment to moment throughout life (in a process generally termed '**re-becoming**'). What is more (in a teaching called *anatta*, or 'non-self'), it is argued that our separate identity is a conventional, rather than an absolute, way of looking at things. Ultimately, everything connects with everything else, and we are not separate from the ever-changing world that surrounds us. In other words, Buddhism sees each person as part of an on-going process, what they *do* now contributes to the future, and what they *are* now is the result of a vast number of actions in the past. What Buddhism warns about is the craving to cling on to this present individual life, which it regards as a selfish and futile attitude, and one that can only lead to disappointment.

> **Key thought**
>
> The very thing Buddhism warns about, as a craving that leads to disappointment, is a strong motivation for some other religious believers – namely the idea that they will cling onto their life in some form beyond the grave.

6 The future of humankind

> **Key question**
>
> Is it possible to specify the future direction of evolution in a way that includes a religious ideal?

Human beings live forwards; they plan what they want to do, seek satisfaction if they feel a lack, and generally act on the basis of intentions. To understand humankind, it is not enough to ask where it came *from*, we should also ask *where it thinks it is going*.

Science produces technology, and technology enables things to be done that formerly would have been impossible – it shapes the future. Science generally claims academic indifference; in other words, you seek knowledge for its own sake, not for the products that can be developed as a result of it. Nevertheless, scientific knowledge leads to technology, and its significance is related to humankind's hopes for its own future.

Science fiction thrives on exploring the potential of science – whether it is the breeding of a new species, space travel between planets, a life made easy by efficient and intelligent robots and so on. Here, imagination stretches what science and technology can deliver, but it also explores questions about what sort of future humankind wants.

> **Key thought**
>
> The study of how genes work gives the prospect of curing disease. We welcome that, because we want people to be healthy. We want that, because we have a view of what human life should be, and that includes the ability to live a full lifespan and to enjoy good health. So the significance of genetics is related to overall views of the nature and purpose of life.

But what future does science predict? Indeed, can it and should it try to predict the future? What is clear from our brief survey is that science has shown that the world is – and always has been – in a state of flux. Heraclitus got it right; you cannot step into the same river twice. Indeed, you cannot wake up in exactly the same universe on two successive mornings. The universe is expanding, and cooling; the cells in your body are reproducing along with their strands of DNA; mutations are taking place, some of which may influence future generations.

Central to the whole awareness of evolution is the sense that all living things, existing on this thin film of life on this planet, hurtling through space in a remarkably empty and inhospitable universe, are related to one another and are bound up in a process of change.

Some thinkers, however, have attempted to go beyond this general sense of the place of humankind within the overall scheme of things, and have tried to specify exactly how the future will develop, attempting to bring the idea of evolution and change in line with a Christian expectation of a definite end point to which the universe is moving.

Teilhard de Chardin sought to reconcile the very positive view of humankind's future that he found within the scientific community with his commitment to the Christian faith. In particular, he believed that Christianity should promote the future of life on Earth, rather than being concerned primarily with some 'spiritual' goal beyond it.

By observation of the way in which early life forms developed, Teilhard came to formulate what he called 'the law of complexity/consciousness'. He considered that at the very basis of the evolutionary process were simple atoms, but these joined with others to become molecules, then joined again to become more complex mega-molecules, like the proteins. Beyond that, even more complex arrangements started to form as cells, and from then on you have increasing complexity as you go up the evolutionary tree of life, finally reaching humankind. Humans have more intelligence and self-awareness than other creatures, because they are the most complex beings yet produced by this process of ever-more-complex, convergent evolution.

The overall principle he saw in this was that *the more complex an organism became, the more consciousness it possessed*. He therefore argued that the process of evolution could be seen as a cone. At the base are individual atoms, then, as these come closer together, you work your way up through molecules and cells, to the emergence of humankind. Then he sees the process continuing up the cone. Just as atoms become part of molecules, so individuals become part of something greater, with Christ appearing as mankind comes together.

Whereas the spreading of life over the limited surface of the planet creates a 'biosphere', so he sees communication and thought spreading over the surface of the Earth and becoming ever more complex, in what he terms the 'noosphere' (from the Greek word for mind). The noosphere cannot expand indefinitely, since the surface of the globe is finite, so humankind comes together (e.g. through increasing communication and travel) until it reaches a point of complete unity, which faith then describes as the universal Christ. He calls this goal of evolution 'Omega'.

Key people

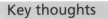

Teilhard de Chardin (1881–1955)
Brought up in a devout Catholic family, but with an overwhelming interest in rocks and fossils, Teilhard became a Jesuit priest but also continued to work as a scientist (researching as a palaeontologist, with a particular interest in tracing early human remains in Europe, Africa and Asia). Apart from his specialist scientific papers, his writings are an attempt to find a Christian vision of the future that would be compatible with what he sensed as a very positive scientific vision of the future. Their publication was banned by the Jesuit order, and only appeared after his death. His best-known book is *The Phenomenon of Man*, written in 1940, but published in 1959.

Key thoughts

Teilhard's basic question was: how can Christ be related to the ultimate goal of the evolution of humankind, such that I can serve him by helping to build the world of tomorrow?

Notice, of course, that this is not Jesus of Nazareth, but the Christ spoken of by St Paul, in Ephesians; the Christ who is to take everything up into himself.

Notice that this attempts to 'locate' the object of religious devotion in a way that fits in with an evolutionary perspective. Just as Aquinas presented God as the 'unmoved mover' lying behind and making possible all that came into existence, so Teilhard effectively places God (in the person of Christ) at the end point of a process of convergent evolution.

A major problem with this sort of theory is that it is a mixture of science and religious vision, and it allows the two sorts of language and proof to flow into one another. Thus his best-known book, *The Phenomenon of Man*, has a great deal of scientific 'evidence' about the progress of evolution, but it also contains religious views about the Universal Christ which cannot be considered as the conclusions of a scientific argument.

Teilhard may therefore be criticised from both a religious point of view (since he appears to make the appearance of the Universal Christ dependent upon a particular view of evolution) and also from a scientific point of view (for trying to reach religious conclusions from scientific evidence, and going beyond what can be proved).

What Teilhard was trying to do was to fuse a scientific view of evolution and the future with the religious need for a personal and spiritual goal. Many might agree that it would be ideal if one's scientific view of the future coincided with one's religious goal, but that is not the same thing as trying to use the one to prove the other.

Summary diagram

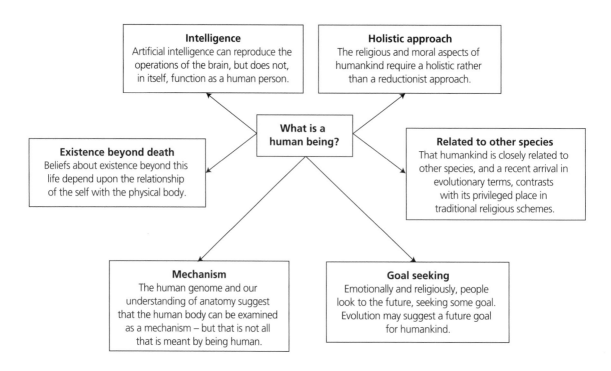

Study guide

By the end of this chapter you should have thought through various aspects of humankind – its origins, the relationship between mind and body, and its possible future, both individual and global – and have an appreciation of what aspects of being human can and cannot be fully described by science.

Revision checklist ✓

Can you explain ...?

- How genetics shows the relationship between humans and other species.
- The difference between taking a *reductionist* and a *holistic* view.
- What is meant by a *functional* analysis (e.g. of a computer system or a human being).

Do you know ...?

- Why a mind is not the same as a brain.
- The difference between immortality and resurrection.
- What Teilhard de Chardin meant by 'complexity consciousness'.

Give arguments for and against ...

- The view that Persinger's helmet can give a genuine religious experience.

Examples of essay questions

1. Evolution and genetics have undermined the privileged place that humankind has within the universe. Discuss.

AO1 This requires a basic understanding of the place of humankind within an evolutionary view, and thus the relationship between humans, other species and the universe of which they are a part.

AO2 This needs to discuss the nature of human 'privilege', the basis upon which it is claimed, and the part it plays in religion.

2. It will never be possible to construct an artificial self. Do you agree?

AO1 In responding to this question, it is important to specify what, if anything, should be considered distinctive or essential about a human person.

AO2 Evaluating this requires a view on what essential aspects of personhood can be linked to a part of the physical anatomy that could conceivably be constructed artificially. Most obviously, it requires a comment on the parallels between the brain and computers.

Further questions

1 Of the various religious views about life beyond death, which (if any) in your view is the most compatible with the scientific view of the self?

2 Discuss the religious implications of the fact that humankind shares many of its genes with other species.

3 To what extent is it valid to link a religious idea to a scientific theory? Illustrate your answer with reference to Teilhard de Chardin's view of evolution leading towards Christ as Omega.

We have only to look at the history of science over the last 400 years to realise that it has the most amazing capacity to surprise.

By the end of the eighteenth century, the predictable world of Newtonian physics was well established and technology had vindicated the scientific method. Then, in the nineteenth century, along came the geologists and then Darwin with his theory of natural selection, and suddenly the world was a far more ancient and complex place than had previously been imagined.

By the end of that century, Haeckel and others could celebrate the triumphs of science, convinced that all the basic groundwork in physics and biology had been established. Then, with the twentieth century came the dramatic changes in physics and cosmology brought about by relativity and quantum mechanics, and biology became revolutionised by the discovery of DNA and its genetic codes.

In the last decades of that century, information technology developed to the point at which the computing power and technology that had enabled men to walk on the moon in the 1960s became almost laughably limited, and instant global communication via the internet became routine. With the twenty-first century, the incorporation of cameras, MP3 players, PDAs and 'sat nav' systems into phones is just one example of technology, the complexity and functionality of which would have been unthinkable a generation earlier.

And the fundamental research side of science also progresses. The quest for the origins of matter and a 'theory of everything' continues. We are constantly discovering that the universe is a stranger and far larger place than previously thought. Between the first and second editions of this book, the estimated number of stars in our own galaxy quadrupled!

And what of religion? At the end of the seventeenth century, Toland saw it being stripped of its metaphysical beliefs, and made rational and compatible with science. At the end of the nineteenth, Haeckel mocked it as superstitious, and looked to a future dominated by rationality and science. Marx predicted that, with the emancipation of the proletariat, it would come to an end, and the implication of much of Freud's work is that healthy individuals do not need it.

Yet, in the twenty-first century, religion persists. A large percentage of the world's population claim to belong to one of the great religions, at least nominally. And those who do not accept formal religion may nevertheless claim some sort of spirituality and moral sense, exploring those issues about the meaning and purpose of human life with which the religious traditions have been concerned.

What is more, any idea that the world is divided into white-coated, utterly rational, long-eared scientists on the one hand, and gullible, spiritual, emotionally naive religious folk on the other, must remain hopelessly inadequate, even as a caricature. Most people think and feel deeply about life and its meaning, just as most people accept and benefit from what science has achieved.

1 Technology and ethics

Science is defined by method – by the systematic use of reason and evidence, and by the critical evaluation and progressive refining or replacement of theories. It is therefore morally neutral. Scientific discoveries can be used for good or evil: the nuclear technology that can provide clean power can also provide the bomb.

By contrast, religion has always been intimately concerned with moral issues, which spring naturally from its view of the nature of human life and its place in the universe. It would therefore be unrealistic to expect religious people to refrain from commenting on the ethical issues raised by science and technology.

Example: Animal–human hybrid embryos

The Human Embryo Fertilisation Bill, set before the UK parliament in the spring of 2008, allowed for the creation of embryos that were the result of inserting the nucleus of an adult human cell into an animal egg. Although described – particularly by opponents of the bill – as part human and part animal, these 'hybrid' embryos would be used for research purposes and would be destroyed within fourteen days, while they were still no more than a bundle of cells.

The idea was that such embryos could provide a good supply of stem cells to be used in research to understand human genetic abnormalities, and thus potentially to find cures for genetic diseases.

The moral argument for the development of hybrid embryos was, first of all, that unless there was a supply of suitable stem cells, research that could potentially prevent human suffering would be frustrated. Secondly, it was argued that the only alternative, if research was to continue, was to use human embryos.

The argument against, as presented by Cardinal Keith O'Brien, head of the Catholic Church in Scotland, was that the creation of hybrids was an affront to human life and human dignity. This view reflects the idea that human life has a unique status, and that the manipulation of life to produce hybrid creatures (albeit allowing them to live for a short period of time) represented an immoral tampering with the normal way of producing new life.

- Both sides of this ethical argument want to enhance human life: those in favour by researching to eliminate the suffering caused by disease; those against by preserving the unique status of a human being.
- Those studying ethical theory will recognise that the first takes a *utilitarian* view, and the second a *natural law* view (for further details of these ethical arguments, see *Ethical Theory* in this series).

One question is absolutely fundamental to the assessment of these two positions: at what point does a unique human life begin? If the microscopic bundle of cells is a person, then a good case can be made for not creating 'hybrid' persons. If not, the stronger case lies with those who see this as a pragmatic solution to the need for material on which to experiment for the greater long-term benefit of those who suffer.

These are ethical and philosophical questions, but they need to be informed by science. Wild images of hybrid creatures and references to 'Frankenstein science' do not help serious debate; science needs to explain the reality of those bundles of cells – what they are and what they are not.

Science and technology therefore throw up an increasing number of questions that cannot be answered from within their own disciplines. However, the fact that science has contributed hugely to human well-being in the past (think of all the features of modern life that would not be possible had it not been for science) means there is the presumption that it will continue to contribute positively. Hence the assumption that is often found within the scientific community that almost all research and technology is valid, and that ethical restraints should only be put in place where proven harm can be shown. Thus, for example, a very polluting technology might well be abandoned because of a general consensus that the environment needs to be protected. However, where such clear harm is not shown – as in the creation and treatment of very early hybrid embryos – there is a tendency for a utilitarian ethic (that one should do that which appears to offer the greatest benefit to the greatest number of people involved) to come down in favour of exploiting the potential of science.

Technology is essential to life in the developed world. However, most people depend upon it without understanding how it works. I have to rely on someone to understand and correctly service the engine of my car; if it goes wrong, I am at a loss. People may fear technology because they feel that they are not able to understand or control it.

Getting beyond a utilitarian view, there are the broad ethical and religious questions about what life is for – and these questions (as in the natural law approach to ethics) rightly address the activities of science and the application of its resulting technologies. That, of course, is beyond the scope of this present book. *But it is crucially important to recognise just what belongs to the realm of religion and what to science.* Religion does *not* have a monopoly on moral thought – that can equally well be done from an entirely secular and rational point of view (as is often argued, particularly by those who take a broadly utilitarian position). On the other hand, science itself does *not* provide moral guidelines for research of technology. Just because something *can* be done does not mean that it *should* be done.

Key thought

DNA testing can show that you have, or have the potential to develop, Huntington's disease, muscular dystrophy, cystic fibrosis and haemophilia. It can also show if you are prone to Alzheimer's disease, hypertension and other conditions. That is a simple scientific fact. But would you want to know, and would you want a life-insurance company to know, if you tested positive? Personal and moral issues of this sort cannot be solved from within the scientific community, but require serious moral thought. Hence the interest in such matters on the part of those who have religious views about the nature and value of human life.

An on-going debate that highlights this is the value and safety of genetically modified (GM) crops. On the one hand there are arguments about crop yields and the ability to resist disease, with the corresponding gains, particularly in areas of the world that are desperate for more effective agriculture. On the other there are concerns about human safety and whether or not genetically modified DNA could transfer to bacteria in the human gut.

On the one hand, there may be no direct evidence of a health risk; on the other, it is difficult to establish whether a rise in allergies to soya can be linked to the import into the UK of GM soya produced in the USA. Clearly, all technology needs to show a clear overall benefit before it is implemented. The decision to implement does not lie with the scientific community, but is political, and therefore should be informed by the public willingness to accept the technology (providing, of course, that the public are sufficiently well informed to be able to make that decision).

Example: A medical application

Within the human body, living cells are being produced all the time, controlled by genetic information. When a mistake occurs, the body normally detects that this has happened, and the cell is destroyed. If, for some reason, the body's immune mechanism fails to detect the error, the cell may grow and reproduce out of control, forming a cancer. At the moment this is treated by removing the malignant cells by surgery, or progressively reducing the cancer by causing a level of damage to all cells, on the assumption that the healthy ones are better able to recover than the malignant ones.

However, it is hoped that, by identifying the gene that produces the protein to inhibit the growth of malignant cells, more effective methods of treatment will be developed, giving patients exactly the right gene proteins to enable their bodies to reject and eliminate the malignant cells.

Fundamental scientific research thus suggests a future for medicine compared with which our present methods may one day seem crude. The impulse to heal and care is not exclusive to religion, even if it is promoted by religion. That puts science and religion on the same side – differences arising only in terms of how best to gain benefit while acknowledging the value of each and every human life.

One problem with any new technology is to know how far to push its application. Genetic modifications to animals are a case in point. In 2007 American scientists established a breeding colony of 500 'supermice', genetically modified to allow them to be more energetic and have greater stamina than ordinary mice. The metabolism gene that was altered is one that mice share with humans. It would be theoretically possible therefore to produce super-athletes. But would that be acceptable? What is the purpose of human life? Should we aim to improve the species by all means possible? These ethical issues touch the fundamental questions of the meaning and purpose of life – and hence enter the sphere of human thought and experience that has traditionally been occupied by religion as well as philosophy.

The moral principles may, of course, be presented in either a secular or a religious context, but it is certainly relevant for a religious perspective (particularly one held by a substantial percentage of a population) to be taken into account in making political and moral decisions about the use of science and technology.

2 The human quest

Science reflects a fundamental quest to know and understand, a quest which itself reflects Aristotle's view that a human being is essentially a thinking animal. In 1926, the philosopher A. N. Whitehead wrote:

> *When we consider what religion is for mankind, and what science is, it is no exaggeration to say that the future course of history depends upon the decisions of this generation as to the relations between them. We have here the two strongest forces (apart from the mere impulse of the various senses) which influence men, and they seem to be set against one another – the force of our religious intuitions, and the force of our impulse to accurate observation and logical deduction.*
>
> (*Science and the Modern World*, 1926)

Key quotes

On the one side there is the law of gravitation, and on the other the contemplation of the beauty of holiness. What one side sees, the other misses; and vice versa.

A. N. WHITEHEAD, *SCIENCE AND THE MODERN WORLD*, 1926

Science is most significant as one of the greatest spiritual adventures that man has yet known.

KARL POPPER, *THE POVERTY OF HISTORICISM*, 1957

Human beings have a great capacity to think, examine and analyse; they also act intuitively, creatively and with a grasp of their place within the whole scheme of things.

Neither religion nor science can benefit from a polarisation in which all the thinking is ascribed to science and all the intuition and feeling to religion. Science needs intuition, imagination and feeling as much as religion needs careful thought and a radical honesty in examining the world.

Sadly, confrontations continue between the shrill arguments of evangelical atheism (which claims to be scientific, but all too often defaults to an unthinking scientism, abandoning reason and evidence in favour of polemic) and those religious believers who are too defensive of traditional doctrines to enter into a fully open discussion of the broadly spiritual dimension of life.

But, as Einstein and others have argued, religion and science may support one another, each contributing to a balanced view of the world what the other lacks. *But that requires the self-confidence of science to recognise the value of the personal and intuitive grasp of reality, and of religion to accept that its traditional beliefs, if taken literally, seldom reflect the full mystery of existence.*

Global warming and the impact of the human species on the natural environment is the absolutely fundamental practical and moral issue of the twenty-first century. An industrialised environment delivers the goods people want, but at a price in terms of the quality of life and the protection of the natural world, upon which our future depends. The traditional debates between science and religion have been about the compatibility of religious beliefs and the scientific understanding of the nature of reality; the debates of the future will need to be about the meaning, purpose and quality of life, and of the role that science and technology can play in delivering what humankind needs if that quality is to be maintained.

GLOSSARY

Alienation a state in which people feel themselves to be deprived of personal achievement and satisfaction.

Anthropic principle the argument that the initial conditions and structure of the universe had to be exactly as they were in order for humankind to develop.

Archetype an image through which individuals participate in the common but profound experiences of their society.

Atomism the theory (first put forward in the fifth century BCE) that all matter is composed of atoms separated by empty space.

Big Bang a popular way of describing the event, about 13.7 billion years ago, that marks the origins of the present known universe.

Cartesian dualism Descartes' distinction between mind (unextended in space and known immediately) and matter (extended in space and known through experience).

Conscious (mind) those things of which we are aware.

Cosmological argument argument for the existence of God based on the regularity and structure of the universe.

Cosmology the study of the nature of the universe as a whole.

Creation science the term used for the range of arguments put forward from about the 1970s to argue for an understanding of nature based on the idea of creation by God, including the idea of intelligent design. Although backed by religious fundamentalism, it claims to be science rather than religion. See also Chapter 7, section 6, for the creationist challenge to evolution by natural selection.

Deduction the process of applying logic in order to establish conclusions from general principles.

Deism the view that the world was created by God, who established the principles under which it should operate, but does not interfere directly in its operation.

Determinism the philosophical view that all things are totally conditioned by antecedent causes, and that future events are therefore theoretically predictable.

Efficient cause that which is the agent of change.

Empiricism the view that all knowledge starts with sense experience.

Epicycle the path traced by a point on the circumference of a circle as that circle is rolled around the circumference of a larger one; used for calculating the orbits of planets up to the seventeenth century.

Existentialism a philosophy relating to the sense of meaning and purpose in human life.

Final cause the purpose of a thing; the actualisation of its essence and potential (in Aristotelian philosophy).

Fine tuning the argument (often associated with the anthropic principle) that the original constants determining the development of the universe are exactly what is needed for the universe to exist.

Form Plato's term for a universal, of which particulars are merely copies.

Functionalism a functionalist view of the mind looks at the process by which the brain receives data, assesses it and then decides what the body should do in response.

Genome the chemical sequence of genetic information strung out along DNA.

Gnostic used of those who claimed secret 'knowledge' as the basis for their religious views.

Heliocentric describes a view that places the Sun (rather than the Earth) at the centre of the cosmos.

Holistic describes an approach, argument or view that considers the functioning of complex entities as a whole, rather than as the sum of their individual parts.

Immanence used of God as found within the world.

Immortality the belief that part of a human being (generally described as the essential self or soul) does not die with the body.

Induction the process of gathering data from observation and experiment in order to establish a general theory or principle.

Instrumentalism the view that scientific laws are to be assessed by the results they yield.

Irreducible complexity the argument that the complexity of organisms cannot be fully explained by examining their constituent parts.

Light year the distance travelled by light in one year, at a speed of 300,000 kilometres per second.

Logical positivism a school of philosophy from the first half of the twentieth century, which, influenced by the success of science, attempted to equate the meaning of a statement with its method of verification.

Methodological naturalism the view that scientific enquiries are limited to observations of this world, and therefore that they cannot deal with the 'supernatural' except in so far as it has a natural component or effect.

Miracle an event deemed to show the direct intervention of God, often seen as a 'violation of a law of nature'.

Model an image, taken from common experience, used in order to explain a phenomenon.

Mysticism the intuitive sense of going beyond the limitations of space and time, and feeling at one with, or at home in, the universe.

Natural philosophy the branch of philosophy which considers the physical world; a term used to include science prior to the eighteenth century.

Neurotheology not a scientific term, but one that refers to the study of brain activity associated with religious experience.

Nihilism the view that the universe is without purpose, but is simply the outworking of mechanical laws that operate under conditions but do not have any 'aim' as such.

Normative one way of describing the relationship between science and religion is to say that science is *descriptive* while religion is *normative*. Normative issues concern the 'norms' or values by which things may be judged.

Noumena things as they are in themselves.

Obsessional neurosis compulsive behaviour stemming from repressed trauma.

Ockham's Razor the principle that one should opt for the simplest explanation; generally summarised as 'causes should not be multiplied beyond necessity'.

Omnipotence the quality of being all powerful; able to do anything (used of God).

Omniscience the quality of being all knowing (used of God).

Panentheism the view that all things exist within God and he within them.

Pantheism the view that the world itself is to be worshipped as God.

Paradigm a theory or complex of theories which together set the parameters of what is accepted as scientifically valid within its particular sphere of study. Kuhn describes how paradigms may eventually be replaced if they prove inadequate.

Phenomena those things which are experienced through the senses; in Kant's view, phenomena are contrasted with *noumena*, or things as they are in themselves.

Pre-conscious (mind) those things that we may not be aware of at this moment, but which we are capable of remembering.

Primary qualities a term used by Locke for those qualities thought to inhere in objects, and are therefore independent of the faculties of the observer (e.g. shape).

Providence the view that God has created the universe in such a way as to provide what is needed for life, and especially for human life.

Rationalism the view that all knowledge starts with the processes of human thought.

Re-becoming the Buddhist view that human beings, like all complex entities, are constantly changing and that there is no fixed self.

Reductionist describes an approach that analyses complex entities into their component parts, with the view that reality lies with the parts rather than the whole.

Reincarnation the belief that a self or soul can pass on to another body after death.

Resurrection the belief that, after death, God raises human beings to life, where they are judged and either rewarded or punished.

Scientism the view that science gives the only valid interpretation of reality.

Secondary qualities a term used by Locke for those qualities used in the description of an object that are determined by the sensory organs of the perceiver (e.g. colour).

Space–time a theoretical point of infinite density and no extension, from which the present universe, including space and time themselves, is thought to have evolved.

Teleological argument an argument for the existence of God, based on the idea of a final end or purpose.

Theism the view of God held by Judaism, Christianity and Islam. God is said to be both within the world and yet transcends it.

TOE a 'theory of everything'; the attempt to find a single theory to account for the four fundamental forces of nature (gravity; electromagnetic; strong nuclear; and weak nuclear).

Transcendence used of God as found beyond the world of sense experience.

Unconscious (mind) the memories of events that we are unable to remember, generally because they are too painful or embarrassing, especially events that took place in the earliest years of life, and which have therefore been repressed.

FURTHER READING

There are a huge number of books relevant to the broad issue of religion and science. A selected list of these is given on the *Access to Religion and Philosophy* website, which includes a range of resources for students, and information about other books in this series.

However, for those who want to set their study of religion and science within the current debate between atheists and religious believers, with particular reference to science, the following are representative:

Collins, Francis, *The Language of God*, Simon & Schuster, 2007
Dawkins, Richard, *The God Delusion*, Bantam Press, 2006
Dennett, Daniel, *Breaking the Spell: Religion as a Natural Phenomenon*, Penguin, 2007
Lennox, John, *God's Undertaker: Has Science Buried God?*, Lion Hudson, 2007
McGrath, Alister, *The Dawkins Delusion*, SPCK, 2007
Stenger, Victor, *God: The Failed Hypothesis*, Prometheus Books, 2007

These books are also valuable as a follow-up to the issues covered in this book. Hopefully, having already considered the basic arguments outlined here, students will be able to engage with both sides of this debate, positively and critically.

Online resources for this book and others in the series

New books and websites are appearing all the time.
Keep up to date and share your own suggestions with other students and teachers.

For suggestions for further reading, comments from the authors
of the *Access to Religion and Philosophy* series and further advice for students and teachers,
log on to the *Access to Religion and Philosophy* website at:

www.philosophyandethics.com

INDEX